DUMB LUCK

Vũ Trọng Phụng (1912–1939)

DUMB LUCK

A Novel by Vũ Trọng Phụng

Peter Zinoman, Editor

Translated by
Nguyễn Nguyệt Cầm and Peter Zinoman,
with an Introduction by Peter Zinoman

ANN ARBOR, THE UNIVERSITY OF MICHIGAN PRESS

Copyright © by the University of Michigan 2002
All rights reserved
Published in the United States of America by
The University of Michigan Press
Manufactured in the United States of America
⊗ Printed on acid-free paper

2005   2004   4 3 2

A CIP catalog record for this book is available from the British Library.

Library of Congress Cataloging-in-Publication Data applied for
ISBN 0-472-06804-0 (paper)

Contents

Contents

Acknowledgments

The publication of this translation of *Số Đỏ* is made possible by permission granted by Vũ Trọng Phụng's son-in-law, Nghiêm Xuân Sơn.

The translation and introduction were completed with financial support provided by the Helman Family Faculty Fund, the University of California Committee on Research, and the University of California Pacific Rim Research Program. The latter grant was secured thanks to the initiative of David Del Testa.

This project remains deeply indebted to Lại Nguyên Ân, who helped to guide our efforts at every stage of the interlinked processes of research, translation, and writing. We have also benefited from extensive advice and support provided by three trail-blazing scholars of Vũ Trọng Phụng's work: Hoàng Thiếu Sơn, Văn Tâm, and Nguyễn Đăng Mạnh. We were fortunate to receive additional assistance in Hanoi from Trần Đăng Thao, Tạ Duy Anh, Hoàng Ngọc Hiến, Nguyễn Công Minh, Thanh Châu, Hà Minh Đức, and Phan Cự Đệ.

Among the friends, colleagues, and family members who read and critiqued drafts of various versions of the manuscript, we especially wish to acknowledge Basil Guy whose keen editorial eye and remarkably detailed suggestions improved the manuscript in numerous ways. We also profited from the constructive comments of John Balaban, Rita Kipp Smith, Craig Reynolds, Vasudha Dalmia, Priya Joshi, Nancy Peluso, Sylvia Tiwon, Christoph Giebel, Micheline Lessard, Liu Xin, and Joy Zinoman. We were touched and energized by Lê Thị Thấm Vân, Keith Taylor, Benedict Anderson, Hazel Hahn, Eva-Lotta Hedman, John Connelly, Irwin Scheiner, Gene Irschick, Andrew Barshay, Anthony Reid, John Whitmore, Công Huyền Tôn Nữ Thị Nha Trang, Yeh Wen-hsin, and Fred Wakeman Jr. As with all of our research and writing on Vietnamese history and literature, this project owes something intangible to the long-term comradeship of Birgit Hussfeld, Hans Schodder, and Jim Carlson.

A special thanks as well to Christopher Goscha and Agathe Larcher, who helped with several tricky problems of translation and facilitated the library and archival research in France upon which much of the introduction is based.

It is impossible to say enough about the role of David Chandler, Ingrid Erickson, and Marcia LaBrenz at the University of Michigan Press. Without their gentle prodding and unflagging encouragement, it is unlikely that this project would ever have been brought to completion.

Finally, we thank our son, Alexander Thiên, for bringing us untold joy utterly unrelated to this project. We close with an expression of gratitude, love, and admiration for our four parents, Nguyễn Công Minh, Lê Thị Kim Chi, Murray Zinoman, and Joy Zinoman.

Introduction

Vũ Trọng Phụng's *Dumb Luck* and the Nature of Vietnamese Modernism

Peter Zinoman

During the late-colonial decade of the 1930s Vũ Trọng Phụng produced a body of writing that stands today as the single most remarkable individual achievement in modern Vietnamese literature. In a
graveside eulogy to the writer delivered in Hanoi on 15 October
1939, the celebrated "new poet" Lưu Trọng Lư likened his late
friend's significance within the literary life of his day to Balzac's role
in nineteenth-century France. "Vũ Trọng Phụng's work exposes and
condemns all that is ugly, corrupt, and grotesque about humankind
during our era," Lư declared. "Vũ Trọng Phụng is to Vũ Trọng
Phụng's era what Balzac was to Balzac's era."[1] Lư's analogy pointed
to obvious affinities between the remarkably panoramic account of
interwar Vietnamese society depicted in Phụng's oeuvre and *The
Human Comedy*'s comprehensive collective portrait of nineteenth-
century France. It also conveyed something of Phụng's extraordinary
productivity. At the time of his death Phụng had completed at least
eight novels, seven plays, five book-length works of nonfiction reportage, several dozen short stories, a handful of lengthy literary
translations, and hundreds of reviews, essays, articles, and editorials.[2] If this inventory of output appears less than Balzacian, it must be
recalled that, when he died from the combined effects of tuberculosis

and opium addiction, Vũ Trọng Phụng was one week shy of his twenty-seventh birthday.

Phụng's acknowledged satirical masterpiece, *Dumb Luck*, was published first in serial form in the *Hanoi Newspaper* (*Hà Nội Báo*) starting on 7 October 1936, five months after the Popular Front took power in France. The electoral victory of the new government—formed through an alliance of Communists, Socialists, and Radicals—abruptly transformed the political climate of French Indochina.[3] Not only were the Socialists and Communists traditional opponents of colonial policy, but the platform of the new government called for a "parliamentary commission to investigate the political, economic, and moral situation in the overseas French territories."[4] Prime Minister Léon Blum placed the Ministry of Colonies in the hands of Marius Moutet, a well-known critic of colonial abuses and advocate of "colonisation altruiste."[5] Hopes for a significant liberalization of colonial policy soared as the newly appointed governor-general, Jules Brévié, promulgated Indochina's first labor code, amnestied thousands of political prisoners, and relaxed censorship. Toward the end of the year scores of strikes broke out involving tens of thousands of workers, and breathless appeals for fundamental political reforms rang out from a newly energized press.[6]

As with all novels, *Dumb Luck* embodies something of the particular time and place in which it was produced. The sunny optimism of its madcap narrative reflects the euphoria with which many Vietnamese greeted the Popular Front victory. Recurring references to "progress" (tiến bộ), "science" (khoa học), "social reform" (cải cách xã hội), "womens' rights" (nữ quyền), "the sporting movement" (phong trào thể thao), "civilization" (văn minh), "modernity" (tân thời), and "Europeanization" (Âu hóa) recall the progressive language and modernizing ethos that dominated public discourse during the era. A widespread obsession with the "common people" (bình dân) and the "popular movement" (phong trào bình dân) illustrate the growth in Indochina of a newly fashionable populist sensibility. *Dumb Luck*'s remarkably diverse cast of characters (roughly thirty in all) reflects the rise during the late colonial era of a colorful array of new social types: the urban vagrant, the professional athlete, the fashion designer, the medical specialist, the avant-garde artist, the foreign-educated student, the crusading journalist, and the "new" woman.

Moreover, *Dumb Luck*'s preoccupation with market relations reflects the acceleration of capitalist development in Indochina during the interwar years. The profit motive animates nearly every character in the novel from the lowliest vagabond to the most idealistic social reformer. The emergence of a predatory business class is dramatized in the character of Victor Ban, with his diversified holdings in brothels, hotels, pharmaceuticals, and venereal disease clinics. Economic metaphors saturate the text as in the depiction of police officers yawning "like merchants during a recession" and greeting a repeat offender "like a regular customer of a family business." Not even religion is exempt from the entrepreneurial spirit of the age as exemplified by the Buddhist monk Tăng Phú's crass efforts to enhance recruitment and donations for his order.

Dumb Luck also reveals an array of quasi-universal sensations—an urban sensibility, a cosmopolitan orientation, a growing skepticism about the transparency and reliability of language, and heightened feelings of irony and impotence—connected to the rapid, unexpected changes that characterize the modern age more generally.[7] While such changes were highlighted during the dramatic early months of the Popular Front era, many Vietnamese had come to perceive them as elements of a permanent existential condition that began with the colonial conquest in the mid-nineteenth century and intensified as a result of tumultuous economic and political transformations during the two decades following World War I. In 1930 a decade-long postwar boom abruptly gave way to violent political confrontations between the colonial state and an array of anticolonial forces followed by intense state repression and punishing years of economic stagnation and decline.[8] For many Vietnamese who lived through these turbulent years, the Popular Front victory was viewed less as a single moment of radical break than as another episode within a new historical trajectory marked by constant rupture and transition—a trajectory that even the colonial state was powerless to control.

Although thoughtful Vietnamese observers were not unaware of the powerful global forces altering their corner of the world during the era, it is not surprising that traditional conceptions of change continued to shape their apprehensions of these modern transformations. Indeed, *Dumb Luck* owes its title to one such conception—the astrological notion of *số* (fate)—which had long provided a framework for most Vietnamese to cope with ordinary and unexpected

3

fluctuations in their lives.[9] *Dumb Luck*'s preoccupation with *số*—embodied in the recurring appearance throughout the narrative of fortune-tellers, omens, and prophesies—suggests an effort to mine Vietnamese tradition for a means to domesticate and make sense of the essentially unpredictable and accidental character of modern life. Indeed, the distinctive character of Vietnamese modernism—defined as the cultural expression of a critical and self-reflexive attitude toward social, political, and economic modernization—may be found in the incongruity of the historical coexistence of traditional epistemologies and modernizing development and by the efforts of Vietnamese intellectuals to discover a suitable aesthetic form to express their subjective experience of this incongruity.

As a pioneering Vietnamese modernist, it is no coincidence that Vũ Trọng Phụng's brief life dovetailed with colonial Indochina's most intense period of social, economic, and political modernization. In addition to having lived through the war, the boom years, the rising tide of anticolonial violence, the Depression, and the victory of the Popular Front, Phụng experienced the radical linguistic and educational changes of the early 1920s, the rapid growth of print capitalism, and the massive influx into Vietnamese society of Western mores and customs. Nor is it surprising that he produced his remarkable body of work from within the heart of Hanoi, the ancient cradle of Vietnamese civilization, which capitalism and the colonial administration were rapidly transforming into a bustling metropolis. Indeed, the turbulent ebb and flow of Phụng's fleeting life, unstable times, and transitory environment provide a revealing window into the origins of *Dumb Luck*'s innovative modernist sensibility.

⟶

Vũ Trọng Phụng was born in Hanoi on 20 October 1912, the only child of working-class parents.[10] His father, Vũ Văn Lân, was the son of a landless village official from the Mỹ Hào district of what was then Hưng Yên Province. As a young man, Phụng's father migrated several hundred kilometers northeast to Hanoi, where he found work as an electrician at the Charles Boillot Garage.[11] Phụng's mother, Phạm Thị Khách, worked as a seamstress after moving to Hanoi from Hoài Đức, a western suburb of the capital located in Hà Đông Province.[12] Like many new rural migrants to the city, Phụng's parents rented a tiny apartment in the 36 Streets, Hanoi's densely

4

populated commercial quarter. Seven months after Phụng's birth his father died from tuberculosis, leaving his mother a widow at the tender age of twenty-one.[13]

In an idiosyncratic study of the writer—part psychobiography, part personal memoir—published in 1941, two years after he died, his close friend Lan Khai suggested that the most influential person in Phụng's life was his mother, who raised and supported him single-handedly following the death of her husband.[14] According to Khai, his mother's selfless devotion to Phụng saved him from a life of "hunger and vagabondage," a comment reflecting traditional Vietnamese anxieties about the likely plight of fatherless boys.[15] As Phụng's medical condition worsened during the late 1930s, visitors to his apartment on Hàng Bạc (Silver) Street observed that it was his mother, and not his wife, who sat at his bedside fanning him late into the evening. "Everyone who visited Phụng's house was struck by the extraordinary love of the widow for her son," Khai remarked, "a love that was both intense and tender."[16] He also praised Phụng's mother for refusing to remarry despite her youth. It is tempting to locate the origins of Phụng's well-known reservations about the "new Vietnamese woman" and conservative fondness for Confucian morality in the traditional model of female virtue provided by his mother. Indeed, his mother's fidelity to her deceased husband stands in sharp contrast to the serial infidelity of the twice-widowed Mrs. Deputy Customs Officer—arguably the most sustained object of ridicule in *Dumb Luck*.

While Phụng's traditional moralism may or may not be connected to the influence of his mother, there is no question that his famously urban literary sensibility grew out of his lifelong residence in the 36 Streets.[17] An indigenous mixed-use urban agglomeration, the 36 Streets comprised a tangle of narrow winding lanes, each named after the single specialized item—sugar, silver, silk, traditional medicine, or votive paper, for example—sold or produced there. Honeycombed behind rows of shop house facades lining the streets were clusters of residential units, storage spaces, workshops, and courtyards for light and ventilation. Broad paved sidewalks separated the streets from the facades and provided the setting for much of the district's spirited social and commercial life. In addition to the bustle of everyday commerce, life on the sidewalk was animated by the daily influx into the 36 Streets of itinerant peddlers, porters, rickshaw pullers, shoe shine boys, pickpockets, prostitutes, policemen, beggars, buskers, tourists, and *flaneurs*. Residential units tended to be small and overcrowded, and hence all manner of private, even intimate, activities took place on the sidewalk in full public view.

Since Phụng lived most of his life in cramped quarters within the 36 Streets, it is not surprising that sidewalk scenes figure prominently in many of his writings; one critic has even referred to *Dumb Luck* as a "sidewalk novel."[18] Indeed, its opening chapter portrays the motley denizens of one stretch of pavement—a fortune-teller, a sugarcane vendor, the owner of a lemonade stand, and Xuân the ball boy—trading gossip, flirting, exchanging headlines, and haggling over prices. Above the din may be heard "the patter of tennis balls and a scorekeeper's voice" ringing out from a nearby tennis club. Not only does the juxtaposition of sidewalk chatter with the sounds of the club embody the dissonant cacophony of city life, but it reflects the promiscuous jumble of social classes that endowed daily life in the 36 Streets with the democratic ambience of urban modernity.

The high profile of poor and underworld elements in the 36 Streets parallels the preoccupation with marginal social groups found in Phụng's nonfiction reportage—prostitutes in *V.D. Clinic* (Lục Xì), gamblers and con-men in *The Man Trap* (Cạm Bẫy Người), domestic workers in *Household Servants* (Cơm Thầy Cơm Cô), and actors in *Clown Make-Up* (Vẽ Nhọ Bôi Hề). The 36 Streets also provided an excellent vantage point to observe the lifestyles and public behavior of rich and famous residents of the city, many of whom served as models for Phụng's fictional characters, including some of the major figures in *Dumb Luck*.[19] Mrs. Deputy Customs Officer, for example, was probably based on Madame Bé Tý, the widow of a French official whose opulent villa—replete with gold statues, rare birds, and monkey cages—was located down the block from Phụng's apartment on Hàng Bạc Street. Victor Ban conjures images of the self-promoting pharmaceutical giant Hồng Khê, while the entrepreneurial monk Tăng Phú resembles Nguyễn Năng Quốc, the founding editor of the glossy Buddhist newspaper the *Torch of Wisdom* (Đuốc Tuệ).

The urban sensibility of *Dumb Luck* also comes across in the way its frenetic narrative and chaotic language embody the pace and feel of city life. Red-Haired Xuân's improbable social ascent in the novel—from ball boy to salesman to doctor to social reformer to tennis champion to politician to national hero—takes place in a mere five months. According to the critic Đỗ Đức Hiểu, *Dumb Luck* conveys the "random and unstable spirit of the city" through the "atonal" cadences of its dialogue, the "abrupt broken rhythms" of its structure, and the repeated use of mood-shifting words and phrases such as *suddenly* (*chợt* and *bỗng*), *accidentally* (*tình cờ*), *at that moment* (*vừa lúc ấy*), and *abruptly* (*đột ngột*).[20] "Vũ Trọng Phụng is Vietnam's most urban writer," Hiểu concludes, "and *Dumb Luck* is a one-hundred percent urban novel."[21]

Phụng's fixation with the urban environment reflects the rapid, metastasizing growth of his native Hanoi during the early twentieth century.[22] Over the course of several decades the colonial state transformed the city from a regional administrative center linked to a small commercial town into an important industrial zone, a commercial hub for Tonkin's abundant mineral wealth, and the political capital of French Indochina. The Bureau of Public Works filled in hundreds of malarial ponds and swamps, destroyed the imperial citadel, laid out a residential French Quarter, built a monumental complex of government buildings, paved and widened the 36 Streets, and introduced electric street-lights and a modern sewage system. It also promoted the circulation of traffic through the city by tearing down the gates fronting each of the 36 Streets, demolishing the Vauban-style fortifications that separated the citadel from the town, and introducing bicycles, trams, automobiles, and rickshaws. During Phụng's childhood and teenage years the sensation of urban transition was intensified by the postwar boom. Economic growth reached record levels in the 1920s, driven by high prices for Indochinese export commodities and a rapid increase in capital investment.[23] With industrial expansion and the growth of an urban service sector, the population of Hanoi almost doubled, from 75,000 in 1921 to 128,000 in 1931.[24] The economy collapsed with the onset of the Depression, but Hanoi's population continued to swell as deteriorating conditions in the countryside forced cultivators off their land. By 1937 over 154,000 people were crammed into the city, including a large floating population of destitute rural migrants.[25] Given these demographic realities, Phụng's characterization of the vagabond Red-Haired Xuân suggests a journalistic representation of a common sociological type as much as a fanciful work of literary imagination.

If Phụng's residence in the rapidly changing heart of the city determined the tone and subject matter of much of his work, his brief educational career was no less important to his development as a writer. Along with his future colleague and fellow writer Vũ Bằng, Phụng studied at the Hàng Vôi lower primary school (grades 4–6) during the early 1920s.[26] Yet, while Bằng continued into upper primary school (grades 7–9) and eventually attended the prestigious Lycée Albert Sarraut later in the decade, Phụng failed his matriculation exams and left school for good around the age of fourteen. Although little is known about Phụng's experience as a student, there is no doubt that it shaped the trajectory of his life and work. Lan Khai claimed that Phụng was unhappy at school, and that bitterness from the experience infected his writings.[27] Fatherless, sickly, and impoverished, Phụng was ill equipped for the modern school culture that emerged in Indochina during the interwar years in which male students vied for status and the affections of their female classmates through displays of wealth and athletic prowess. For Khai, Phụng's well-documented contempt for the preoccupations of Vietnamese youth—sports, romantic love, money, and Western fashions—derived from his failure to fit in socially at school.[28] Moreover, the fact that he left school early distinguished Phụng from his bitterest literary rivals—the members of the Self-Strength Literary Group (Tự Lực Văn Đoàn)—many of whom had earned postgraduate degrees or studied in France. Phụng's disdain for his more highly educated competitors is revealed in *Dumb Luck*'s absurd depiction of "High School Graduate Tân" and Mr. Civilization (Văn Minh), who "displayed a contempt for foreign diplomas common among Vietnamese students who had returned from six or seven years in France without ever actually earning one."

What limited education Phụng did receive was shaped by the fact that he entered school shortly after Governor-General Albert Sarraut introduced radical educational reforms into Indochina in 1918.[29] Most important, Phụng benefited from a new policy that waived tuition for public schooling during the first six years of instruction. Had he been born into similar social and economic circumstances a decade earlier, Phụng likely would have remained illiterate or at best functionally literate in Chinese characters. Instead, he was among the first generation of northern Vietnamese students to receive primary instruction exclusively in French and in the recently adopted romanized Vietnamese script known as *quốc ngữ*. As a consequence,

Phụng and his peers acquired a cultural orientation radically different from that of every previous generation of northern Vietnamese intellectuals.

Prior to the French conquest of Indochina, most Vietnamese writing, including all government documents, was composed in classical Chinese.[30] To render the native tongue in written form, primarily for expressive and literary purposes, the Vietnamese employed another character-based writing system known as *chữ nôm*. The fact that facility with *chữ nôm* was predicated on a prior knowledge of Chinese ensured that large segments of the Vietnamese elite were fluent in Chinese and culturally sinocentric. This orientation was intensified through the gradual adoption by the precolonial elite of key elements of Chinese bureaucratic government—the civil service examinations most significantly, along with a parallel educational curriculum structured around the study of classical Chinese texts. Given their educational backgrounds and language capabilities, it is not surprising that early anticolonial Vietnamese intellectuals sought escape from the colonial predicament in easy to access Chinese and Japanese models of cultural self-strengthening.[31] French cognizance of this fact, combined with a widespread perception that ideographic writing systems prevented economic and scientific development, provided the main impetus for the colonial state to substitute instruction in French and *quốc ngữ* for the traditional curriculum in characters.[32]

The radical nature of colonial language policy nourished at least three characteristically modernist orientations within important segments of the Vietnamese elite and emergent intelligentsia. The first was a historicist feeling of living in totally novel times—a feeling that originated with colonialism and the early effects of capitalist development but that was intensified significantly by the abrupt linguistic transformation.[33] In "An Era of Poetry" (Một Thời Đại Trong Thi Ca), published during 1941, the talented brothers Hoài Thanh and Hoài Chân examined the emergence of this historicist sensation and underlined its relation to literary production during the colonial period.[34] In this important essay they suggested that the "form and spirit" of Vietnamese society had remained fundamentally unchanged during the thousand years prior to the mid-nineteenth century. With the colonial conquest, however, Vietnamese history had experienced a dramatic break, the extent of which was as sweeping as its encounter with China at the start of the first millennium. "It feels as if fifty centuries of change have occurred in fifty years," the authors wrote. "We now live in western houses, sport western hats, walk in western shoes, and wear western clothes. We use electric lights, clocks, cars, trains, and bicycles."[35] Hoài Thanh and Hoài Chân then linked these changes in material life ("how we live") to changes in ideology ("how we think"). As families vied to enroll their children in the new colonial schools, characters gave way to *quốc ngữ*, and Montesqieu and Voltaire replaced Confucius. Finally, the authors described transformations in emotional life ("how we feel")—changes that, as they put it, "penetrated into the deepest part of our souls." The remainder of the essay addressed this third kind of change—what Hoài Thanh and Hoài Chân called a "new rhythm of emotion"—and its literary manifestation in the "new poetry" movement.[36]

In *Dumb Luck* recurring references to the conflict over "the old" and "the new" reflect the historicist preoccupation with the radical novelty of the present that saturated Vietnamese society during the interwar years. In the opening chapter Red-Haired Xuân expresses disdain for "old-fashioned professions such as peanut vending, fruit picking, or running errands for actors." Officers at the police station complain that the recent modernization of Vietnamese domestic life is depressing their arrest records. Discussions over the funeral of Grandpa Hồng's father reveal divided opinions about the contemporary relevance of "traditional and modern rites." The frequency of suicide attempts at White Bamboo Lake is depicted as a "contemporary barometer of the tragic conflict between the Old and the New." Likewise, the narrator describes an argument between Mr. Civilization and his mother as "another episode in the never-ending conflict that split all families down the middle: the clash between the Old and the New." In these examples the modernism of Phụng's recurring invocation of the historicist theme is reinforced by the self-reflexive cynicism that he adopts toward his society's obsession with historicism.

Colonial language policy also functioned to endow the new Vietnamese elite with a Eurocentric cosmopolitanism. Within a single generation not only were most educated Vietnamese unable to read Chinese or Japanese, but they were incapable of reading anything that any Vietnamese had written during the previous two millennia (with the exception of a select handful of works laboriously translated into French or *quốc ngữ*). Also important was the fact that this first generation of Vietnamese educated in *quốc ngữ* was necessarily faced with the absence of a textual tradition in the romanized script. Coupled with their inability to read characters, intellectually ambitious members of the interwar elite were left with little choice but to immerse themselves in the literary traditions of France and its European neighbors.

Phụng was no exception. In newspaper articles he cited Zola, Hugo, Malraux, Dostoyevsky, and Gorky as major influences.[37] At nineteen he prefaced his first major published work, the play *No Echo,* with an epigraph from Zola.[38] During his early twenties he completed translations of Victor Hugo's *Lucrecia Borgia* and *The Last Days of a Condemned Man.* Later in the decade he likened accusations that his work was pornographic to historical controversies over the writing of Flaubert, Baudelaire, Colette, and Victor Margueritte.[39] His newspaper columns include casual references to the homosexuality of Gide and Verlaine, to formal differences between French and Russian social realism, and to fashionable metropolitan literary journals such as *Les Nouvelles Litteraires.* Phụng's cosmopolitanism may also be located in his engagement with Freudian psychology. Although *Dumb Luck* mocks the Vietnamese elite's superficial understanding of the great Viennese modernist, Phụng was fascinated by Freudian character analysis and attempted to employ it in several of his works.[40] "No one in our group followed international developments as closely as Vũ Trọng Phụng," remarked Vũ Bằng, "or tried as hard to understand the obscure terms that we read in *Le Canard Enchainé.*"[41]

Critics have suggested a variety of Western models for the distinctive style and structure of *Dumb Luck.* In the early 1940s Vũ Ngọc Phan argued that its mode of broad comedy recalled the slapstick humor of Charlie Chaplin, a suggestive analogy, since Red-Haired Xuân is hired to impersonate the silent screen star in one of the novel's flashbacks.[42] During the 1950s both Thiều Quang and Nguyễn Mạnh Tường likened *Dumb Luck* to the farcical comedies of Molière, many of which had been translated into Vietnamese and staged in Indochina during the 1920s and 1930s.[43] Most recently, Hoàng Thiếu Sơn has compared the lighthearted tone and looping trajectory of the novel to the picaresque narratives of Cervantes, Rabelais, Dickens, and Gogol, writers with whom Phụng was certainly familiar.[44] Structural

11

comparisons may also be made to Balzac's *Illusions perdues*, the story of a provincial boy's abrupt ascent through the social hierarchy of nineteenth-century Paris.[45]

An intriguing nonliterary point of reference is *Le roi des resquilleurs* (The King of the Wanglers), a popular French film released in 1930 that dramatized the adventures of a street-smart urban trickster named Bouboule, who "rises to success through a series of uncanny strokes of luck and wiliness."[46] Reflecting a preoccupation with the figure of the "little guy" in French popular culture after World War I, Bouboule was an "irrepressible, mocking, slang-speaking, rebellious Parisian" who exhibits a kind of craftiness based on "showing up the ineffectiveness of authorities and systems of control."[47] As in *Dumb Luck*, many of the film's key events take place at sporting events such as bicycle races and boxing matches. In a final scene, strikingly reminiscent of the penultimate chapter of *Dumb Luck*, Bouboule becomes the unwitting hero of a France-England rugby match, is hailed as a national savior, and marries the woman of his dreams. Red-Haired Xuân, of course, enjoys an identical fate after his performance in the Indochina-Siam tennis tournament.

Le roi des resquilleurs spawned successful sequels in 1931, 1933, and 1938 and some or all of them may well have been shown in Indochina. If *Dumb Luck* was indeed a novelization of the film adapted to the Indochinese environment, it is tempting to consider what there was about it that made Phụng imagine that it might appeal to his Vietnamese audience. Perhaps he recognized the potential of the film's madcap absurdism to strike a chord with an urban population undergoing rapid, unpredictable modernization. Alternatively, he may have sensed that the image of the little guy who triumphs through craftiness and good fortune resonated with a sympathy for feisty underdogs felt by a Vietnamese elite whose own cultural identity had been shaped by a long history of struggle against a hegemonic China.[48] The enduring affection of Vietnamese readers for *Dumb Luck* may also be linked to Charles Rearick's argument that the French found the "fast-paced buffoonery" of the *Le roi des resquilleurs* "a welcome antidote to the worries of the emergent Depression."[49] Following its publication in 1936, *Dumb Luck*'s unflagging popularity throughout seventy-five subsequent years of anticolonial struggle, world war, civil war, and social revolution may

12

reflect its escapist appeal for a demoralized and deeply insecure population.

In contrast to interpretations of the novel that emphasize its relationship to Western models, the critic Văn Tâm has highlighted *Dumb Luck*'s debt to influences from indigenous popular culture.[50] He argues, for example, that the novel's reliance on punning, double entendre, and a form of humorous, mutually misunderstood conversation known as "he says chicken she says duck" (*ông nói gà, bà nói vịt*) recall common conventions of traditional *chèo* opera.[51] Moreover, Tâm identifies a host of compelling similarities between Red-Haired Xuân and Master Pig (*Trạng Lợn*), a fortunate dunce whose bawdy misadventures feature prominently in a popular collection of Vietnamese folktales. It is no coincidence that Tâm's effort to locate *Dumb Luck* within a tradition of indigenous folk culture occurred in northern Vietnam during the late 1950s, a period in which Party critics were compelled to denigrate works exhibiting excessive foreign influence. As a minor participant in the Vietnamese Hundred Flowers Movement that agitated against government censorship during the era, Tâm's effort to link *Dumb Luck* to indigenous traditions may have been part of an ultimately unsuccessful gambit to prevent the banning of the novel. Nevertheless, the similarities he highlights between *Dumb Luck* and traditional narratives are suggestive and recall that, while colonial language policy worked to sever interwar writers from their own high cultural canon, it did not prevent their continued engagement with a traditional popular culture that was primarily oral in nature. It was this ongoing engagement with premodern traditions and the local environment, together with the penetration of modernizing, global forces into Indochina, that gave Vietnamese modernism its distinctive character.

In addition to engendering historicism and cosmopolitanism, another effect of the linguistic transformation in Indochina was to generate anxiety about the reliability of language in general and the unstable relationship between language and power. Because the precolonial system created a homology between the acquisition of power and fluency in Chinese, the abrupt abandonment of characters raised troubling questions about how power in colonial society might be attained. This anxiety was intensified by the rapid influx of unfamiliar discourses into Indochina, each promising to replace the Chinese classics as guides for the achievement of power and prosperity: the discourses of social reform and mass politics, the discourses of science and medicine, the discourses of modern love and romance, and the new literary, philosophical, and poetic discourses. Much of the humor in *Dumb Luck* comes from Red-Haired Xuân's uncomprehending initial reaction to these modern discourses followed by his unexpected public demonstration of mastery over them. While Xuân's capacity to impersonate a doctor, a fashion designer, a politician, a professional athlete, a journalist, and a poet points to the Vietnamese elite's weak grasp of the languages spoken by these modern figures, it also reveals the inability of these new, unfamiliar languages to provide an accurate indicator of social standing.

Xuân's success in the novel is also a product of his genuine mastery over an additional modern discourse: the discourse of advertising. Xuân's checkered employment history included jobs as a peanut vendor, newspaper hawker, and broadcaster of commercials for venereal disease treatment. When, in the course of the narrative, he is subsequently forced to demonstrate command over an unfamiliar modern discourse—such as medicine, new poetry, or politics—Xuân meets the challenge by employing skills and experience that he acquired during his career in advertising. For example, he steels his nerves prior to delivering a virtuoso speech at the opening of the new tennis court by reminding himself that he "had always been effective using his voice to conquer, oppress, and move the hearts of the masses—whether selling peanuts, working as an advertising boy at the theater, or making loudspeaker announcements for the King of Cochinchinese Venereal Disease Treatment." At the Fairyland Hotel, Xuân defeats his rival in an impromptu poetry contest by modifying the "jingles that he had recited flawlessly by heart in the past, back when he chanted advertisements over a loudspeaker for Victor Ban." Xuân's advertising skills also come in handy when he tries to calm the angry crowd after the tennis tournament: "Using talents he had developed advertising venereal disease medicine," the narrator explains, "Red-Haired Xuân won over the public just like a skillful French politician."

These episodes point to Phụng's belief that the supra-discourse of modern advertising had replaced the wisdom of the ancients as a kind of skeleton key to success and happiness in the modern world. "This is the era of advertising," he once told his close friend Nguyễn

Triệu Luật. "Anyone who ignores this will be eliminated even if they have talent and training."[52] In *Dumb Luck* the power of advertising is underscored by its broad utility in all conceivable circumstances—economic, social, political, artistic, romantic, and scientific—and by its apparent substructural relationship to every other form of modern discourse. Reference to the hegemony of advertising may even be seen located in the novel's unusual sloganeering chapter headings, which the critic Võ Thị Quỳnh likens to a form of "publicity used to attract customers."[53] Coupled with the inherent untrustworthiness of advertising as a mode of communication, its insidious proliferation throughout society signaled the growing unreliability of language in general during the interwar years.

—

After leaving school, Phụng worked briefly as a clerk at the Godart Department Store before landing a secretarial position with the Imprimerie D'Extrême Orient (IDEO), his first job in the publishing industry.[54] According to Vũ Bằng, whose uncle also worked at the IDEO, Phụng was a quiet employee who spent his idle time writing or reading French newspapers such as *Le Monde* or *Le Canard Enchaîné*.[55] Although his uncle claimed that Phụng was eventually fired for writing on the sly during working hours, Bằng believed that Phụng quit to protest the obsequious behavior of his coworkers toward their French superiors. Both stories may be apocryphal. As Nguyễn Đăng Mạnh points out, Phụng probably lost his job at the start of 1930 during a wave of white-collar layoffs triggered by the onset of the Great Depression.[56]

The claim that Phụng had already started writing while employed at the IDEO finds support in a memoir by Tam Lang, who was then working on the editorial board of *Hà Thành Ngọ Báo* (Capital Daily News), a Hanoi daily published by Bùi Xuân Học.[57] Sometime around 1930 Tam Lang received an unsolicited short story from Phụng that centered around a melancholy conversation between a childless couple. Tam Lang was impressed with the story and published it in the following issue. Thereafter he received several more stories from Phụng but was discouraged from printing them owing to their prurient subject matter. Weeks later Phụng called upon Tam Lang at the newspaper office, told him that he was dissatisfied with his job at the IDEO, and expressed a desire to apply for an editorial position at *Hà Thành Ngọ Báo*. Since none were available, he hired Phụng as a clerk-typist but was forced to let him go soon after for chronic lateness. Nevertheless, Phụng remained loosely connected to the newspaper, publishing a handful of additional short stories there in 1931 and 1932.[58]

Hà Thành Ngọ Báo was a heady place to work during the early 1930s. Under the guidance of Hoàng Tích Chu and Đỗ Văn—francophone intellectuals who had studied in Paris during the mid-1920s—*Hà Thành Ngọ Báo* was the first *quốc ngữ* daily in Tonkin to follow journalistic practices and maintain production qualities consistent with metropolitan standards.[59] As its editor-in-chief, Hoàng Tích Chu placed the coverage and presentation of hard news at the core of the newspaper's journalistic mission.[60] This contrasted with its major northern rivals—*Thực Nghiệp* (Commerce and Industry), *Khai Hóa* (Enlightment Daily), *Trung Bắc* (North-Central Review), and *Nam Phong* (Southern Wind)—which were dominated by didactic essays, translations of Western literature, and reprints from southern publications. Another modern innovation of Chu was to promote coverage of what Phụng referred to as "the seamy side of life."[61] To this end he spearheaded what became an influential journalistic movement of first-person realist reportage by commissioning and publishing Tam Lang's brilliant *I Pulled a Rickshaw* (Tôi Kéo Xe) in early 1932. Chu was also the first editor from the north to promote writing that eschewed the stilted conventions of traditional prose such as parallel sentences, flowery metaphors, and the excessive use of Sino-Vietnamese words. Instead, he advocated a spare and straightforward style that quickly became something of a standard for the northern Vietnamese press.[62] Due to the influence of Đỗ Văn, who had apprenticed as a printer in Paris, the newspaper was among the first in Tonkin to be laid out in a Western style, with narrow, vertical rectangular columns beneath eye-catching headlines. Recalling the novelty of the newspaper decades later, Vũ Bằng explained that he "only began to enjoy newspapers around the time that Hoàng Tích Chu and Đỗ Văn . . . first wrote for *Hà Thành Ngọ Báo*."[63]

Phụng's experience at *Hà Thành Ngọ Báo* was instrumental to his development as a writer. Not only did its editors publish his first short stories, but they provided a model of urban living, cosmopolitanism and modern journalistic practice to which Phụng remained committed for the remainder of his career. According to Vũ Bằng, Hoàng Tích

Chu and Đỗ Văn impressed the young writers at *Hà Thành Ngọ Báo* as embodiments of "the movements for new living, new thinking, new eating and drinking, and new forms of struggle."[64] Phụng's famously succinct and earthy writing style and his much vaunted preoccupation with the urban underclass may also be traced to the influence of Hoàng Tích Chu. After observing up close the commotion generated by Tam Lang's reportage during the early 1930s, Phụng devoted considerable energy to the genre throughout his career, eventually earning the nickname "the King of Reportage." In a brief article about *Hà Thành Ngọ Báo* published in 1935, Phụng described his time at the paper as the "glorious days when Hoàng Tích Chu was still there" and "readers anticipated the noon-time publication of the paper like lovers waiting for each other in the park."[65]

Equally important were the connections that Phụng made at *Hà Thành Ngọ Báo* with fellow journalists—connections that helped him find work at dozens of newspapers throughout the decade and that gradually coalesced into a far-flung community of friends and colleagues.[66] The fluid trajectory of Phụng's career reflects the explosive growth of Indochinese journalism during the 1930s. While only thirty periodicals in *quốc ngữ* came out during the first sixty years of French rule (1862–1918), Sarraut's language reforms created a robust market for *quốc ngữ* publications, especially newspapers.[67] Indeed, the French sociologist André Dumarest identified a taste for newspapers as a defining cultural feature of the new elite that emerged in Indochinese cities during the interwar years.[68] To meet the surging demand, publishers founded over forty *quốc ngữ* periodicals between 1926 and 1930 and another four hundred during the 1930s.[69] These included general interest newspapers as well as specialized publications focusing on literature, science, sports, cinema, women's issues, and fashion. This growth in publishing generated demand for written material, which facilitated the transformation of writing into a profession. Editors during this period paid as much as five piasters for an essay or short story, enough for productive and popular writers to make a modest living.[70]

The fact that Phụng began his career as a writer during a period marked by the commercialization of the Indochinese press contributed to the modern sensibility of his work. The logic of the market encouraged a modernist emphasis on originality and innovation. But it also subjected Phụng to the tyranny of public opinion and middle-class tastes, which in turn provoked expressions of cynicism, persecution, and impotence—attitudes characteristic of an embattled avant-garde.[71] Through recurring references to the business side of journalism and the arts, *Dumb Luck* highlighted the commodification and alienation of writers, artists, and intellectuals in Indochina during the era. For example, the wickedly satirical conversation between Mr. ILL and an unnamed journalist outside the European Tailor Shop calls attention to the tendency of capitalism to create a gulf between self-important cultural producers and a faceless public. The gist of their exchange is a shared expression of contempt for the low level of their audience. "It is simply a waste of breath to talk about art with the people," the journalist complains. In the next scene the journalist's pathetic attempt to sell advertising space to Mrs. Civilization underscores his own subordination to market forces. Moreover, the journalist's argument that attacks on his paper by conservative forces are enhancing its commercial appeal highlights the remarkable capacity of colonial capitalism to transform even political controversy into a kind of commodity. As with Phụng's historicist sensibility, his clear-eyed recognition that intellectual and artistic life was being commodified by colonial capitalism is less striking than his mocking characterization of the self-righteous contempt of artists and intellectuals like himself toward their own commodified condition.

Dumb Luck's concern with the emergence of modernity in Indochina extends to its assault on the Self-Strength Literary Group and the project of cultural modernization that it promoted. Founded in 1932 by Nhất Linh—a former employee of the Bureau of Finance who dabbled in drawing at the Indochinese Fine Arts Institute and studied chemistry and physics at Montpellier—the Self-Strength Group emerged as the most influential commercial publishing venture in Tonkin throughout the 1930s.[72] In addition to its two weeklies—*Phong Hóa* (Mores) and *Ngày Nay* (These Days)—the group founded the Đời Nay Publishing House, which reprinted the novels, poetry, and reportage first published in the journals. Other core members included the novelist Khái Hưng, the fashion designer Lemur, and the new poets Thế Lữ, Xuân Diệu, and Huy Cận. Linh's talented younger brothers, Thạch Lam and Hoàng Đạo, helped run the journals and wrote much of the literature and criticism that appeared in their pages.

The original mission of the group was defined in contradistinction to the conservative cultural project of *Nam Phong,* a journal funded by the state between 1917 and 1934 and edited by the prominent neotraditionalist Phạm Quỳnh.[73] It advocated the creation of a new Vietnamese culture through the selective adoption of Western values combined with the preservation of a "natural essence," closely linked in the mind of Phạm Quỳnh to the Sino-Vietnamese Confucian tradition. Dismissing Phạm Quỳnh's vision as unrealistic and old-fashioned, the youthful, French-educated, and largely middle-class leaders of the Self-Strength Group promoted a radical, unattenuated Westernization of Vietnamese society. Their program was expressed obliquely in their fiction and poetry and advanced directly in a succinct manifesto written by Hoàng Đạo entitled *Ten Points to Bear in Mind* (*Mười điều tâm niệm*).

(1) Modernize completely, without hesitation, and modernization means Westernization; (2) Have faith in progress, believe that things can get better; (3) Live according to ideals; (4) Work for the good of society; (5) Train your character; (6) Encourage women to go out in the world; (7) Acquire a scientific mind; (8) Value real achievement, not careerism; (9) Exercise and strengthen your body; (10) Learn to organize your work methodically.[74]

Many of the characters in *Dumb Luck* can be read as caricatures of the leaders of the Self-Strength Group or of the "modern" individuals whom they celebrated in their work. Mr. ILL bears an obvious resemblance to Nguyễn Cát Tường (aka Lemur), the designer who invented the modern *áo dài* and wrote a trend-setting fashion column for *Phong Hóa.* With his useless French education and fainthearted desire to "reform society within the prevailing legal framework," Mr. Civilization recalls Nhất Linh and his brothers. The character of Miss Snow lampoons the frivolous "modern woman," addicted to dancing and romantic love, who dominated the novels and advice columns published by the group. Her unrequited suitor—the "short young man with glassy eyes, an emaciated body, and the gaunt face of a poet"—represents a parody of the avant-gardist new poets. Nguyễn Thành Thi has identified the maudlin quatrain that he offers to Snow at the Fairyland Hotel as a direct satire of Thái Can's *Chiều Thu* (Autumn Afternoon), first published in *Phong Hóa* during 1935.[75]

Moreover, *Dumb Luck* offers a point-by-point refutation of Hoàng Đạo's manifesto. It ridicules the obsessive invocation of modernization, Europeanization, and progress by members of the Self-Strength Group. It suggests that their do-gooding idealism frequently masked commercial motives. It exposes the prurient self-interest animating their promotion of women's liberation. It mocks their shallow understanding of science and fashionable preoccupation with sports. It pokes fun at their ingrained elitism and underscores the opportunism of their newfound support for the "people."

Phụng's ideological opposition to the Self-Strength Group was reinforced by commercial rivalry and class resentment. Given his hard-won, autodidactic knowledge of metropolitan life, it is no surprise that Phụng resented Nhất Linh's effortless cosmopolitanism, born of elite schooling and firsthand experience in France. The Self-Strength Literary Group invited this resentment by affecting a flamboyant snobbery exemplified in a catty column in *Phong Hóa* and *Ngày Nay* that combed rival newspapers for factual mistakes, grammatical errors, and opinions considered erroneous or old-fashioned. The longevity, excellent production qualities, and cool sophistication of *Phong Hóa* and *Ngày Nay* contrasted with many of the feisty, fly-by-night journals with which Phụng was associated and must have fed his bitterness. When several journals belonging to Vũ Đình Long's *Tân Dân* Publishing House emerged to challenge the commercial hegemony of the Self-Strength Literary Group during the late 1930s, Phụng went to work for them and eventually came to be considered a member of the *Tân Dân* Group.[76] In 1937 he engaged in a spirited "pen war" with *Ngày Nay* columnist Nhất Chi Mai over the latter's charges that *V.D. Clinic, Household Servants,* and *The Storm* were pornographic.[77] Indeed, *Ngày Nay*'s attack on Phụng may have been triggered by *Dumb Luck*'s mocking portrayal of the Self-Strength Group during the previous year.

Although Phụng's hostility to the Self-Strength Group helps explain *Dumb Luck*'s bitter attack on modernizing and Westernizing reformism, it does not permit a neat characterization of his ideological proclivities or political sympathies. On one hand, his reservations about rapid Westernization have led to charges of cultural conservatism. In 1942 the budding Marxist Vũ Ngọc Phan labeled him a "reactionary" for "dismissing all progressive movements without offering alternatives."[78] Likewise, Trương Tửu argued that *Dumb Luck*'s attack on frivolous "romantic" fads such as dancing, fashion, and free love represented a conservative attempt to protect "morality, justice and culture" and to save those "tricked into crime, gambling and debauchery."[79] Yet, *Dumb Luck*'s ridiculous description of the monarchist Joseph Thiết, the neotraditionalist Society for Spiritual and Ethical Development (Hội Khai Trí Tiến Đức), and colonial officialdom disclosed little sympathy for conservative political alternatives. Moreover, the explicit sexuality and preoccupation with the underclass found in his work contrasted with the prudishness and elitism of existing conservative projects. Phụng was also skeptical about unorthodox forms of traditionalism linked to organized religion or Eastern spiritualism, as evidenced by his caustic portrayals of the monk Tăng Phú, the fortune-teller, and the two battling herbalists.

Phụng's relation to the Left was equally problematic. He shared the Indochinese Communist Party's (ICP) anticolonialism, contempt for the nouveau riche, and commitment to "realism," but he showed little admiration for the Communists and never joined the Party. Adopting a position borrowed from the European left, Trương Tửu compared Phụng—with his cultural conservatism, hostility to the bourgeoisie, and outraged social conscience—to Balzac, whose Catholicism and Monarchism did not hinder his capacity to portray society "realistically."[80] But Phụng's understanding of "realist" literature—work based on "what the eye sees and the ear hears" coupled with a vague sense of concern with the poor and downtrodden—contrasted with Communist definitions of the concept especially in the Party's later Stalinist incarnations. Phụng's preoccupation with social outcasts and the criminal underclass, instead of workers or peasants, for example, disappointed Communist critics, as did his frequent use of infantile sexuality rather than class struggle as a device to motivate characters. Following the Moscow show trials, Phụng denounced Stalinism in print and belittled orthodox Vietnamese Communists whose fidelity to Moscow he likened to the Self-Strength Group's faddish devotion to foreign movements.[81] While this suggests the possibility that Phụng's primary political commitments were nationalist, he expressed no interest in any of the nationalist parties of the 1930s such as the Việt Nam Quốc Dân Đảng or the Constitutionalists.

On the other hand, Lan Khai argued that his friend was fundamentally apolitical and nonideological. What drove Phụng, Khai claimed, was an angry nihilistic pessimism, a psychological consequence of his poverty and illness.[82] In the final analysis Phụng's skepticism toward government, politics, and religion and his refusal to identify clearly with any particular partisan group suggests the jaded cynicism of the modern journalist.

●

Fifteen years after his death, in the wake of the Geneva Accords (1954), Phụng's work emerged almost immediately within the newly established Communist Democratic Republic of Vietnam as an object of intense public scrutiny. This renewed attention was occasioned by the promotion of his work by the founders of *Nhân Văn* (Humanities) and *Giai Phẩm* (Literary Selections), journals associated with a short-lived domestic movement for enhanced democracy and artistic freedom—a kind of northern Vietnamese Hundred Flowers Movement—that the Party tolerated briefly before suppressing in 1958.[83] Not only did the leaders of the movement reprint several of Vũ Trọng Phụng's novels, but in 1956 they published a short collection of testimonials suggestively entitled *Vũ Trọng Phụng Is With Us* (*Vũ Trọng Phụng với chúng ta*).[84]

In June 1960, two years after the suppression of *Nhân Văn / Giai Phẩm* by the Party, politburo member Hoàng Văn Hoan—one of the twelve most powerful men in the Democratic Republic of Vietnam—submitted to the journal *Literary Research* (Tạp Chí Nghiên Cứu Văn Học) a twenty-page essay entitled "Thoughts on the Problem of Vũ Trọng Phụng within Vietnamese Literature" (Một Vài Ý Kiến Về Tác Phẩm Vũ Trọng Phụng Trong Văn Học Việt Nam).[85] The essay dismissed the literary significance of Vũ Trọng Phụng's three most popular novels—*The Storm* (Giông Tố), *Dumb Luck*, and *The Dike Breaks* (Vỡ Đê)—and raised suspicions about his political orientation by calling derisive attention to the fact that his novels had been promoted publicly by the "Nhân Văn / Giai Phẩm Clique."

> The *Nhân Văn Giai Phẩm* Clique bypassed the controls of our cultural institutions to republish thousands of copies of Vũ Trọng Phụng's novels, distribute them widely among the population and use them as teaching material in school literature departments. The purpose of this effort was to prove that only pre-revolutionary literature had value and that after the revolution, under the leadership of the Party,

22

writers were forced to serve politics . . . Hence, writers lost their freedom and literature lost its soul. They argued that a genius like Vũ
Trọng Phụng needed neither the revolution nor the leadership of the
Party to produce great work. They claimed that Vũ Trọng Phụng was
our most brilliant realist writer, that he died with the era but that his
work will live forever in the history of our literature. They said that Vũ
Trọng Phụng was a master of the literary world and that he was even
more revolutionary than the Party.[86]

Hoan's essay—charging guilt by association—circulated widely
among cultural officials and sealed Phụng's reputation as a writer
with dangerous counterrevolutionary tendencies. As a result,
Phụng's work was banned in the Democratic Republic of Vietnam
(DRV) during the following twenty-five years and throughout the
unified Socialist Republic of Vietnam (SRV) from 1975 until the onset
of the liberal Renovation (Đổi Mới) policy in the mid-1980s.

Although Phụng's precocious brilliance is widely recognized today, his controversial political reputation has delayed the development of critical interpretations of his work. Even in the non-
communist Republic of Vietnam (RVN), where Phụng continued to
be read between 1954 and 1975, critics devoted little sustained attention to his cultural or political significance. Since the Renovation
policy lifted the ban on Phụng in 1986, critics in Vietnam have carried out a major reappraisal of his work. Because it remains preoccupied with the recent suppression of his writing, however, much of
the new criticism has focused on exonerating Phụng by highlighting
affinities between his work and the historical project of the Communist Party.

This essay seeks to take the recent reappraisal of Phụng in a
different direction by suggesting that his significance lies in a radically modernist sensibility found in his work—a sensibility most
clearly illustrated in the novel *Dumb Luck*. Just as certain formal
features and thematic preoccupations of *Dumb Luck* support this
characterization, the Vietnamese Communist Party's suppression of
the novel strengthens the case for a modernist reading. Like their
counterparts in China and the Soviet Union, Communist Vietnamese literary officials have always dismissed aesthetic modernism as a
uniquely Western form of cultural decadence. In the cultural manifesto entitled "Marxism and Vietnamese Culture" (1948) Trường

23

Chinh described modernist movements such as "cubism, impressionism, surrealism and dadaism" as "gaudy mushrooms" that "sprout from the rotten wood of imperialist culture."[87] Of course, the fact that the Party supressed Phụng for over twenty-five years does not automatically make him a modernist, for it also attacked the works of writers considered to be neotraditionalists, bourgeois reformists, nationalists, and Trotskyists. It is easy to imagine, however, how *Dumb Luck*'s radical and indiscriminate "attitude of questioning the present"—a fundamental element of modernism, according to Dilip Gaonkar—might be read as subversive by a Communist political system that has always treated literature as a morale-building instrument of state policy.[88] Although *Dumb Luck* was banned because literary dissidents promoted it for their own ends during the late 1950s, its irreverent modernist critique of all established institutions and authorities prefigured its dramatic fall from official favor. Unfortunately, the continuing hostility of Communist cultural orthodoxy toward aesthetic modernism has discouraged northern Vietnamese literary criticism from considering its relation to the novel, and debates about Phụng's work today rarely stray from assessments of the relative prominence of (positive) "critical realist" and (pejorative) "romantic" or "naturalistic" impulses in his writings. This essay has suggested, however, that the capacious category of modernism is better able to capture the countervailing elements found in his huge, diverse body of work and, in particular, the remarkable tone, thematic preoccupations, and formal innovations of *Dumb Luck*.

NOTES

1. The eulogy was printed in *Tiểu Thuyết Thứ Bảy* (Saturday novel), no. 284 (11 November 1939): 7–10.

2. A bibliography of Phụng's work may be found in Trần Hữu Tá, ed., *Nhà Văn Vũ Trọng Phụng Với Chúng Ta* (The writer Vũ Trọng Phụng is with us), (Ho Chi Minh City: NXB Thành Phố Hồ Chí Minh, 1999), 8–10. Twenty-five newly discovered pieces by Vũ Trọng Phụng (including plays, short stories, reportage, articles, and editorials) have been published in Vũ Trọng Phụng, *Vẽ Nhọ Bôi Hề: Những Tác Phẩm Mới Tìm Thấy Năm 2000* (Clown makeup: works newly found in the year 2000), comp. Peter Zinoman, annotated by Lại Nguyên Ân (Hanoi: Hội Nhà Văn, 2000). An additional dozen short stories were rediscovered in October 2000 by Lại Nguyên Ân.

3. For the Popular Front's colonial policy, see W. B. Cohen, "The Colonial Policy of the Popular Front," *French Historical Studies* 7, 3 (1972): 368–93.

4. Huynh Kim Khanh, *Vietnamese Communism, 1925–1945* (Ithaca: Cornell University Press, 1982), 209.

5. Panivong Norindr, "The Popular Front's Colonial Policies in Indochina: Reassessing the Popular Front's 'Colonisation Altruiste,'" in *French Colonial Empire and the Popular Front: Hope and Disillusion,* ed. Tony Chafer and Amanda Sackur (London: Macmillan, 1999), 231.

6. Huynh Kim Khanh, *Vietnamese Communism,* 205–18.

7. Marshall Berman, *All That Is Solid Melts in Air: The Experience of Modernity* (New York: Simon and Schuster, 1982).

8. For a survey of these events, see William Duiker, *The Rise of Nationalism in Vietnam, 1900–1941* (Ithaca: Cornell University Press, 1976).

9. The timing and nature of mundane episodes of the life cycle—birth, marriage, and death, for example—are manifestations of *số* as are the onset of unexpected tragedies such as illness or crop failure.

10. According to his birth certificate, Phụng was born in 1913, but Văn Tâm suggests that his parents changed the date in order to get him into school. This is probably correct, since Phụng's childhood nickname, Tý, indicates that he was born during the Year of the Rat in 1912. Văn Tâm, *Vũ Trọng Phụng: Nhà Văn Hiện Thực* (Vũ Trọng Phụng: realist writer) (Hanoi: Kim Đức, 1957), 61. Greg Lockhart mistakenly states that he was born in December. Greg Lockhart, ed., *The Light of the Capital: Three Modern Vietnamese Classics* (Kuala Lumpur: Oxford University Press, 1996), 121.

11. Ngô Tất Tố claims that Phụng's grandfather was once the village mayor (*lý trưởng*) but that his father was a simple villager. Ngô Tất Tố, "Gia Thế Ông Vũ Trọng Phụng" (Vũ Trọng Phụng's family situation), *Tao Đàn: Số Đặc Biệt Về Vũ Trọng Phụng* (Special number on Vũ Trọng Phụng), no. 1 (December 1939): 25.

12. Văn Tâm, *Vũ Trọng Phụng: Nhà Văn Hiện Thực,* 60–61.

13. Thiết Can claimed that Phụng's father died when he was three. Vũ Ngọc Phan, *Những Năm Tháng Ấy: Hồi Ký* (Those months and years: a memoir) (Westminster: Hồng Lĩnh, 1993), 299.

14. Lan Khai, *Vũ Trọng Phụng: Mớ Tài Liệu Cho Văn Sử Việt Nam* (Vũ Trọng Phụng: documenting a Vietnamese literary history) (Hanoi: Minh Phụng, 1941).

15. Ibid., 3.

16. Ibid., 4.

17. For recent discussions of the history of the 36 Streets, see William Logan, *Hanoi: Biography of a City* (Seattle: University of Washington Press, 2000); and Mark Sidel, *Old Hanoi* (Kuala Lumpur: Oxford University Press, 1998), 1–30. See also Christian Pedelahore, "Constituent Elements of Hanoi City," *Vietnamese Studies* 12 (1982): 105–59; and William Logan, "Hanoi Townscape: Symbolic Imagery in Vietnam's Capital," in *Cultural Identity and Urban Change in Southeast Asia,* ed. M. Askew and William Logan (Melbourne: Deakin University Press, 1994), 43–69.

18. Sidewalk scenes recur throughout the novel, such as Great-Grandpa's funeral, the parade for the Siamese king, and the encounter between Mr. ILL and his workers outside of the Europeanization Tailor Shop. Đỗ Đức Hiểu, "Những Lớp Sóng Ngôn Từ Trong 'Số Đỏ' Của Vũ Trọng Phụng" (Waves of Language in Vũ Trọng Phụng's "Dumb Luck"), in Trần Hữu Tá, *Nhà Văn Vũ Trọng Phụng Với Chúng Ta,* 417.

19. Suggestions of real-life models for many of *Dumb Luck*'s characters may be found in Hoài Anh, "Vũ Trọng Phụng, Nhà Hóa Học Của Những Tính Cách" (Vũ

Trọng Phụng, chemist of character), in *Vũ Trọng Phụng—Tài Năng Và Sự Thật* (Vũ Trọng Phụng, genius and truth), ed. Lại Nguyên Ân (Hanoi: Văn Học, 1997), 145–54.

20. Đỗ Đức Hiểu, "Những Lớp Sóng Ngôn Từ Trong 'Số Đỏ' Của Vũ Trọng Phụng," 421.

21. Ibid., 417.

22. Prior to the French conquest, Hanoi consisted of two lightly populated and relatively unintegrated components: a citadel containing administrative offices and residences for imperial troops and officials and the 36 Streets, which functioned as a market town that served the population of the citadel and nearby villages. Circulation throughout the city was restricted by Vaubaun-style fortifications segregating the citadel from the town and by gates that divided each of the thirty-six streets from another. For the colonial transformation of Hanoi, see Gwendolyn Wright, *The Politics of Design in French Colonial Urbanism* (Chicago: University of Chicago Press, 1991), 161–234.

23. Charles Robequain, *The Economic Development of French Indo-China* (London: Oxford University Press, 1944), 158–67.

24. Ng Shui Meng, *The Population of Indochina: Some Preliminary Observations* (Singapore: Institute of Southeast Asian Studies, Field Report Series no. 7, 1974), 41.

25. Claudius Madrolle, *Indochine du Nord: Tonkin, Annam, Laos,* vol. 1 (Paris: Hachette, 1923).

26. Vũ Bằng, "Cái Tài Cái Tật của Vũ Trọng Phụng" (The talents and failings of Vũ Trọng Phụng), in *Văn Học* (Saigon), no. 114 (1970): 31.

27. Lan Khai, *Vũ Trọng Phụng*, 14.

28. Ibid.

29. Gail P. Kelly, *Franco-Vietnamese Schools, 1918–1938: Regional Development and Implications for National Integration* (Madison: Center for Southeast Asian Studies, University of Wisconsin–Madison, Wisconsin Papers on Southeast Asia no. 6, 1982).

30. The precolonial educational and writing systems are discussed in Alexander Woodside, *Vietnam and the Chinese Model: A Comparative Study of Vietnamese and Chinese Government in the First Half of the Nineteenth Century* (Cambridge: Harvard University Press, 1971), 169–233.

31. David Marr, *Vietnamese Anticolonialism, 1885–1925* (Berkeley: University of California Press, 1971).

32. Colonial language policy is discussed extensively in John DeFrancis, *Colonialism and Language Policy in Viet Nam* (The Hague: Mouton, 1977); and Milton Osborne, *The French Presence in Cochinchina and Cambodia: Rule and Response, 1859–1905* (Ithaca: Cornell University Press, 1969).

33. On the relationship between modernism and historicism, see Malcolm Bradbury and James McFarlane, "The Name and Nature of Modernism," *Modernism: A Guide to European Literature, 1890–1930* (New York: Penguin, 1991), 22.

34. Hoài Thanh and Hoài Chân, "Một Thời Đại Trong Thi Ca," in *Thi Nhân Việt Nam, 1932–1941* (Vietnamese poets) (1942; rpt., Hanoi: Văn Học, 1999), 15–47.

35. Ibid., 16.

36. Ibid.

37. Vũ Trọng Phụng, "Để Đáp Lại Báo Ngày Nay: Dâm Hay Không Dâm" (A response to Ngày Nay Newspaper: pornographic or not), *Báo Tương Lai*, 25 March 1937.

38. The epigraph read: "Planter enfin le veritable drame humain au milieu des mensonges ridicules." See *Không Một Tiếng Vang* in *Tuyển Tập Vũ Trọng Phụng* (Collected works of Vũ Trọng Phụng), ed. Nguyễn Đăng Mạnh, (Hanoi: NXB Vân Học, 1987), 1:63.

39. Vũ Trọng Phụng, "Chung Quanh Thiên Phóng Sự Lục Sì" (Around the reportage V. D. clinic), *Báo Tương Lai*, 11 March 1937.

40. See Phụng's *Làm Đĩ* (To be a whore) (1936; rpt., Hanoi: Văn Học, 1996). Phụng's interest in Freud is discussed in Hoàng Thiếu Sơn's introduction to the new edition of the novel entitled "'Làm Đĩ': Cuốn Sách Có Trách Nhiệm Và Đầy Nhân Đạo" ("To Be a Whore": A responsible book full of humanity).

41. Vũ Bằng: "Cái Tài, Cái Tật Của Vũ Trọng Phụng," 38.

42. Vũ Ngọc Phan, *Nhà Văn Hiện Đại: Phê Bình Văn Học* (Modern writers: literary criticism) (1942; rpt., Ho Chi Minh City: Văn Học, 1994), 1:530.

43. Nguyễn Mạnh Tường, "Nhớ Vũ Trọng Phụng" (Remembering Vũ Trọng Phụng), *Vũ Trọng Phụng Với Chúng Ta* (Vũ Trọng Phụng is with us) (Hanoi: Minh Đức, 1956), 5; and Thiều Quang, "Chút Ít Tài Liệu Về Vũ Trọng Phụng" (A few documents on Vũ Trọng Phụng), *Tập San Phê Bình: Số Đặc Biệt Về Vũ Trọng Phụng, Đời Sống và Con Người*, no. 5 (1957): 3.

44. Hoàng Thiếu Sơn, "Số Đỏ: Cuốn 'Truyện Bợm' Kỳ Tài" (Dumb Luck, an extraordinary "story of cunning"), in *Nhà Văn Vũ Trọng Phụng Với Chúng Ta*, ed. Trần Hữu Tá. (Ho Chi Minh City: Ho Chi Minh City Publishing House, 1999), 393.

45. I am indebted to Basil Guy for bringing this to my attention.

46. Charles Rearick, *The French in Love and War: Popular Culture in the Era of the World Wars* (New Haven: Yale University Press, 1997), 139.

47. Ibid., 141.

48. Truong Buu Lam, *Patterns of Vietnamese Response to Foreign Intervention: 1858–1900* (New Haven: Southeast Asian Studies, Yale University, 1967).

49. Rearick, *French in Love and War*, 141.

50. This was first put forward in Văn Tâm, *Vũ Trọng Phụng: Nhà Văn Hiện Thực*, 97.

51. Văn Tâm, "Vũ Trọng Phụng Trong Rừng Cười Nhiệt Đới" (Vũ Trọng Phụng in the tropical jungle of laughter), in Trần Hữu Tá, *Nhà Văn Vũ Trọng Phụng Với Chúng Ta*, 375.

52. Nguyễn Triệu Luật, "Vũ Trọng Phụng Với Tôi" (Vũ Trọng Phụng with Me), *Tao Đàn: Số Đặc Biệt Về Vũ Trọng Phụng*, no. 1 (December 1939): 39.

53. Võ Thị Quỳnh, "Số Đỏ Và Sự Phá Sản Của Ngôn Ngữ" (Dumb luck and the bankruptcy of language), in Lại Nguyên Ân, *Vũ Trọng Phụng: Tài Năng Và Sự Thật*, 131.

54. Lan Khai, *Vũ Trọng Phụng: Mớ Tài Liệu Cho Văn Sử Việt Nam*, 5.

55. Vũ Bằng, "Cái Tài Cái Tật của Vũ Trọng Phụng," 31.

56. Nguyễn Đăng Mạnh, "Tiểu Sử Vũ Trọng Phụng" (short biography of Vũ Trọng Phụng) in Nguyễn Đăng Mạnh, *Tuyển Tập Vũ Trọng Phụng, Tập I*, 10.

57. Tam Lang, "Vài Kỷ Niệm Về Vũ Trọng Phụng" (Memories of Vũ Trọng Phụng), *Tao Đàn: Số Đặc Biệt Về Vũ Trọng Phụng*, no. 1 (December 1999): 54–61.

58. For a discussion of the *Ngọ Báo* stories, see Lại Nguyên Ân, "Những phát hiện mới về tác phẩm của Vũ Trọng Phụng" (New discoveries of work by Vũ Trọng Phụng), *Tạp Chí Nhà Văn*, February 2001.

59. Nguyễn Công Hoan, *Đời Viết Văn Của Tôi* (My life as a writer) (Hanoi: Văn Học, 1971), 94; Thiều Quang, "Chút Ít Tài Liệu Về Vũ Trọng Phụng," 10.

60. For more on Hoàng Tích Chu, see "Hoàng Tích Chu và Lối Văn Học Của Anh" (Hoàng Tích Chu and his succinct writing style), in Vũ Ngọc Phan, *Những Năm Tháng Ấy: Hồi Ký*, 236–46.

61. Phụng mentions Hoàng Tích Chu's fascination with the "seamy side of life" at the end of *Household Servants*. See the Greg Lockhart translation in *The Light of the Capital: Three Modern Vietnamese Classics* (Kuala Lumpur: Oxford University Press), 156.

62. According to his friend Đào Trinh Nhất, Chu's efforts to introduce modern journalism into Tonkin grew out of an intense admiration for the French press: "While studying with him in Paris during 1927, I observed that Hoàng Tích Chu was obsessed with the *Quotidien*, one of the most attractive and well-written newspapers in the French capital. Even when he was short of money for food, Chu always managed to scrounge up five sou for the *Quotidien*. He admired the popular daily column of Pierre Betrand, whose writing he found skillful, clear and full of ideas. He also liked the fact that Bertrand's sentences ran for only one or two lines and that his longest articles never covered more than half a column. Hoàng used to say to me: 'When we return home, we must strive to revolutionize our prose in this way.'" Mộc Khuê, *Ba Mươi Năm Văn Học* (Thirty years of literature) (Hanoi: Tân Việt, 1941), 18.

63. Vũ Bằng, *Bốn Mươi Năm Nói Láo* (Saigon: Phạm-Quang-Khải, 1969), 22.

64. Ibid., 28.

65. Vũ Trọng Phụng, "Phê-Bình Báo-Chí: *Ngọ-Báo*" (Criticizing newspapers: Ngọ Báo), *Tiến Hóa*, no. 3 (7 December 1935).

66. After falling out with Bùi Xuân Học late in 1932, Hoàng Tích Chu and Đỗ Văn eventually moved to a journal named *Nhật Tân* (New Day), where they were joined by much of their old staff from *Hà Thành Ngọ Báo*: Tam Lang, Phùng Tất Đắc, Tạ Đình Bích, Phùng Bảo Thạch, and Vũ Trọng Phụng. The prolific novelist Nguyễn Công Hoan worked there as well. Following a brief stint at Vũ Liên's *Nông Công Thương* (Agriculture, Industry, Commerce), Phụng returned in 1934 to work for his old boss, Bùi Xuân Học, on an irreverent new weekly named *Loa* (Trumpet). There he again worked alongside Tam Lang and the critic and theorist Trương Tửu, who became a close friend and great admirer of his work. While writing for *Loa*, he published occasional pieces in *Phụ Nữ Thời Đàm* (Current Women's Talk), a women's newspaper edited by the brilliant man of letters Phan Khôi. Later that year he moved to the port city of Hải Phòng, where he joined forces again with Phùng Bảo Thạch to run *Hải Phòng Tuần Báo* (Haiphong Weekly). Returning to Hanoi in early 1935, Phụng teamed up once more with Vũ Bằng, Vũ Liên, and Phùng Bảo Thạch to found a short-lived paper named *Công Dân* (Citizen). They added Ngô Tất Tố and Nguyễn Triệu Luật before the venture folded at the end of the year. Phụng moved to Lê Cường's *Hà Nội Báo* (Hanoi Newspaper) in 1936, where he published *The Storm* (*Giông Tố*) and *Dumb Luck* in rapid succession. He was joined there by old comrades—Phan Khôi, Nguyễn Công Hoan, and Trương Tửu—and a host of talented new colleagues including Lưu Trọng Lư and Lê Tràng Kiều. That same year Phụng published major works in *Tương Lai* (The Future)—a newspaper run by his old friends Phùng Bảo Thạch, Ngô Tất Tố, and Vũ Bằng—and occasional pieces in *Ích Hữu* (Useful Friend), a new journal founded by the publishing magnate Vũ Đình Long that included Nguyễn Công Hoan on its staff. Phụng spent much of 1937 working for two papers—*Đông Dương Tạp Chí* (Indochina Times) and *Tiểu Thuyết Thứ Năm* (Thursday Novel)—

which were owned by his old boss from *Hà Nội Báo,* Lê Cường. During the last year of his life he wrote primarily for Vũ Đình Long's *Tiểu Thuyết Thứ Bảy* (Saturday Novel) and *Tao Đàn* (Literary Circle). At the time of his death in 1939, Phụng was poised to embark on a new journalistic venture—a *quốc ngữ* humor magazine under the editorship of Vũ Bằng.

67. DeFrancis, *Colonialism and Language Policy in Viet Nam,* 213.

68. Shawn McHale, "Printing and Power: Vietnamese Debates over Women's Place in Society, 1918–1934," in *Essays into Vietnamese Pasts,* ed. Keith Taylor and John Whitmore (Ithaca: Cornell University Southeast Asia Program, 1995), 177.

69. De Francis, *Colonialism and Language Policy in Vietnam,* 217.

70. Interview with Professor Nguyễn Đăng Mạnh, Hanoi, 21 December 1996.

71. See Eugene Lunn, *Marxism and Modernism: A Historical Study of Lukàcs, Brecht, Benjamin, and Adorno* (Berkeley: University of California Press, 1982), 37–42.

72. For background on Nhất Linh and the Self-Strength Group, consult the following: Stephen O'Harrow, "Some Background Notes on Nhat Linh (Nguyen Tuong Tam)," *France-Asie/Asia* 22, no. 2 (2e trimestre 1968): 205–20; Greg Lockhart, "Broken Journey: Nhat Linh's *Going to France,*" *East Asian History* 8 (1994): 73–95; and Nhật Thịnh, *Chân Dung Nhất Linh* (Portrait of Nhất Linh) (Saigon: Sống Mới, 1971).

73. Hue-Tam Ho Tai, *Radicalism and the Origins of the Vietnamese Revolution* (Cambridge: Harvard University Press, 1992), 46–52.

74. Huynh Sanh Thong, "Main Trends of Vietnamese Literature between the Two World Wars," *Vietnam Forum* 3 (Winter–Spring 1984): 113.

75. Nguyễn Thành Thi, "Thơ 'Thật,' Thơ 'Giả' và . . . Cái Nhếch Mép Của Họ Vũ" (Real poem, fake poem, and the smile of Mr. Vũ), in Lại Nguyên Ân, *Vũ Trọng Phụng—Tài Năng và Sự Thật,* 141–42.

76. Ngọc Giao, "Chủ Nhà In, Nhà Xuất Bản Tân Dân, Ông Vũ Đình Long" (Chief of the Tân Dân publishing house, Mr. Vũ Đình Long), *Tạp Chí Văn Học,* no. 1, 247, January 1991, 58–61.

77. The exchange has been reprinted in Lại Nguyên Ân, *Vũ Trọng Phụng—Tài Năng và Sự Thật,* 205–31.

78. Vũ Ngọc Phan, *Nhà Văn Hiện Đại,* 533.

79. Trương Tửu, "Địa Vị Của Vũ Trọng Phụng Trong Văn Học Việt Nam Cận Đại" (Position of Vũ Trọng Phụng in modern Vietnamese literature), in *Tao Đàn: Số Đặc Biệt Về Vũ Trọng Phụng,* no. 1 (December 1939): 6.

80. Ibid., 7.

81. Một Tay Cách Mệnh Cộng Sản (pseud., Vũ Trọng Phụng), "Lời Hiệu-Triệu Của Một Tay Sịt-Ta-Li-Nít: Đả Đảo Tên Tờ-rốt-kýt Huỳnh Văn Phương," *Tiểu Thuyết Thứ Năm,* no. 13, 14 August 1938, 5. Vũ Trọng Phụng, "Nhân Sự Chia Rẽ Đệ Tam và Đệ Tứ," *Đông Dương Tạp Chí,* no. 20, 21 September-October 1937.

82. Lan Khai, *Vũ Trọng Phụng: Mớ Tài Liệu Cho Văn Sử Việt Nam,* 12–24.

83. See Georges Boudarel, *Cent fleurs ecloses dans la nuit du Vietnam: communisme et dissidence, 1954–56* (Paris: Jacques Bertoin, 1991).

84. Đào Duy Anh, Hoàng Cầm, Phan Khôi, Sỹ Ngọc, Nguyễn Mạnh Tường, Văn Tâm, and Trương Tửu, *Vũ Trọng Phụng Với Chúng Ta,* (Hanoi: NXB Minh Đức, 1956).

85. The essay was first published in 1994 in *Vũ Trọng Phụng: Con Người Và Tác Phẩm* (Vũ Trọng Phụng: life and work), ed. Nguyễn Hoành Khung and Lại Nguyên Ân (Hanoi: NXB Hội Nhà Văn, 1994), 219–45.

86. Hoàng Văn Hoan, 220–21.

87. Trường Chinh, *Selected Writings* (Hanoi: Foreign Languages Publishing House, 1977), 225.

88. Dilip Parameshwar Gaonkar, "On Alternative Modernities," *Public Culture* 11, no. 1 (Winter 1999): 13.

Dumb Luck

by Vũ Trọng Phụng

Originally published in serial form as Số Đỏ in Hà Nội Báo (Hanoi newspaper) beginning on 7 October 1936.

Note on Translation

Số Đỏ was written in *quốc ngữ*, the romanized script that became the dominant language of written communication among ethnic Vietnamese during the early twentieth century. The appearance of numerous French words in the novel reflects the transformation of the Vietnamese language under the influence of French colonialism. The novel also contains many representations of direct speech in which the French language is rendered using *quốc ngữ* transliteration. In all cases such *quốc ngữ* transliterations of French are used to represent the speech of Vietnamese who speak French and serve to reveal the cultural pretensions and poor pronunciation of the novel's francophone Vietnamese characters. Given the obvious symbolic and thematic significance of *quốc ngữ* transliterations within the novel and the fact that Vũ Trọng Phụng used this device in order to capture the actual sounds of his character's voices, we have decided to leave them in the text essentially unchanged. For readers unfamiliar with the phonetic system of *quốc ngữ*, we have provided French and English translations of the transliterations in footnotes at the bottom of the page. We also use footnotes to explain obscure references and to call attention to contextual, historical factors that inform the narrative.

Chapter 1

Red-Haired Xuân's Luck in Love

▸

Mr. and Mrs. Civilization

▸

The Compassion of Mrs. Deputy Customs Officer

Thursday at 3:00 P.M.

Inside the tree-lined tennis stadium two Frenchmen served and volleyed at the net on the far-left court. A pair of ball boys ambled lethargically back and forth, retrieving and returning loose balls. The players swung their rackets lazily, their shirts soaked through with perspiration.

"Xanh ca!"[1]

"Xanh xit!"[2]

The patter of tennis balls and the scorekeeper's voice rang out rhythmically against the humming of tens of thousands of cicadas.

Outside on the street a lemonade vendor squatted against the handles of his cart to talk business with a fellow street merchant.

"Damn! How come it's so dead on Thursday?"

"It's still early. Anyway, I hear that from now on they'll be playing every day, not just on Thursday, Saturday, or Sunday."

"Really! How do you know?"

"C'mon! I hear that in three or four months the king plans to

---

1. *Cinq-quatre* (five-four).
2. *Cinq-six* (five-six).

show up with a huge trophy *Cúp*[3] for the winner of some tournament. . . . They're going to be practicing their asses off!"

On the sidewalk, under the shadow of a kapok tree, an elderly fortune-teller sat quietly, arranging the tools of his trade: a small box, an ink jar, a tube of lipstick, a pencil holder, and several sample horoscope charts. From time to time he yawned, taking on the expression of a true philosopher. Nearby, Red-Haired Xuân attempted to engage a sugarcane girl in deep discussion. Commerce? No! Here we have a budding love affair. And not just any ordinary love affair. It is—as today's newspapers might call it—a love affair of the common People (with a capital *P*).

Extending his hand rudely, Red-Haired Xuân requested a little love . . .

"One-track mind!" she scolded him.

"C'mon. Let's have a little. Just a tiny bit!"

"Pervert!"

"Hey, you're not gonna lose it if you use it."

"True, and saving it doesn't mean they'll worship it either. But, we're not meant to be, and there's nothing in it for me. Nothing's moving today. You buy squat and bring me nothing but bad luck."

Red-Haired Xuân rose abruptly to his feet and admonished her in a voice both sulky and heroic.

"I don't need this crap!"

Miss Sugar Cane shot him a bitchy scowl.

"Hey, if you don't need it, then beat it!"

Chuckling like a whinnying horse, Red-Haired Xuân sat back down.

"I'm kidding. I'm kidding. Of course I need you! We need each other! Take it easy. Give me a *xu*'s worth of sugarcane."

"Money, please . . ."

Reaching into his back pocket, Red-Haired Xuân pulled out a small handkerchief, knotted like a pig's ear. He unfolded it, took out a coin, and tossed it down dramatically onto the cement pavement. As Miss Sugar Cane selected and peeled a stalk for him, Xuân began muttering under his breath.

"Five *hào*. Let's see . . . Two left over . . . I spent three last night

---

3. *Coupe* (cup).

on my buddy. Two *hào* for tickets to the nightclub, one for two bowls of noodle soup with extra-rare beef. Do I know how to enjoy life or what?! A hell-raiser, that's what I am! Eating and throwing money around like that . . . God damn it! But don't worry. Once you agree to move in with me . . . of course I'll stop this reckless spending . . . You never listen, do you . . . ?"

But Miss Sugar Cane didn't reply. Xuân chomped noisily on his stalk. He sucked the sweet juice and spit out the leftover shards in the direction of a nearby electrical pole. Finally, he wiped his hands on his pants, stood up, and stretched his back. Miss Sugar Cane held out nineteen cents in change, but Xuân clasped his hands behind his back.

"Right in the front pocket, my dear . . . Slip those fingers in here!"

Glaring angrily, Miss Sugar Cane opened her fingers and watched as the coins tumbled to the pavement. Xuân bent down quickly to pick them up.

"God damn my mother's milk!"

Recalling the words of a southern opera, Xuân broke into song: "All alone on an autumn night, my tender heart is sinking."

Xuân sashayed over to the fortune-teller. Stopping abruptly, he eyeballed the old man like a peasant discovering Madame Bé Tý's famous monkey cages for the first time.[4]

"Read my fortune! Short term," he blurted out.

Roused from his nap, the old man peered up at Xuân and, quick as a policeman writing a ticket, drew a feathered pen from behind his ear.

"Two *hào*. Two *hào* per reading. Take it or leave it . . ."

"One *hào*. Better than nothing."

"Deal! Where's the money?"

"Here. What do I need with it anyway. . . ."

Crouching down on a mat, Xuân placed a coin before the fortune-teller. The old man unfolded a small piece of tissue paper, ground a bit of powder from his ink stick, and spit purposefully into a small ink pot.

"Date of birth?"

---

4. A well-known Vietnamese widow of a French official whose opulent mansion outfitted with a small zoo was located on Hàng Bạc Street during the 1930s.

"I'm twenty-five, old man. Born the fifteenth day of the tenth month around the hour when the chickens start to sleep."

The fortune-teller leaned forward on his haunches, mumbled pensively to himself, and calculated something on his fingers. Red-Haired Xuân wrapped his arms around his knees and rested his chin on his wrists. The fortune-teller scribbled a few notes and began chanting some astrological verse.

Bad stars becloud your personal fate.
Your parents have passed the earthly state.
They wait with fairies in the nether-world.

He stopped chanting.

"If the time of birth you gave me is correct, then your parents must have died when you were still young."

"Yes! Yes, that's right!"

"Your childhood was filled with hardships."

"It was!"

"Yet, I see that your fate is not totally dark."

He continued to chant:

Propitious stars seem close at hand.
Your name will ring throughout the land.
Fame and the good life are in store for you.

"Great! When do they start?"

"This year. From this year onward, your fate is looking up."

"I've seen no sign of it yet."

"By the end of the year, you'll see."

Xuân was suspicious.

"How has my fate been so far this year?" he asked.

"Up till now, you've been lucky only in *love*."

"How do you mean?"

"The stars suggest that women find you irresistible."

Red-Haired Xuân clapped his hands together as if applauding a well-hit tennis ball.

"Yes! Yes! Yesterday after the show, I passed Sầm Công Lane, and a group of young ladies loitering on the corner charged toward me.[5]

---

5. A small lane in the 36 Streets, located at the center of the red-light district.

They grabbed my hands and pulled at my shirt. I must be hot stuff! You're right on target, old man!"

He turned and sneered at Miss Sugar Cane.

"See!"

Lowering his voice, he whispered to the old man. "Great going! I've got her right where I want her. Your prophesies are worth the price!"

Just then, a sleek automobile pulled up in front of the tennis stadium. The back door opened, and out stepped a hefty woman in her mid-forties, made up like a fashionable young seductress. Her face was caked with powder and lipstick, and her newly permed jet-black hair fell in tiny ringlets from beneath an elegant and equally tiny scarf. She looked to be over seventy kilograms! She clutched a huge leather purse and a tiny umbrella in one hand, and in the other she hugged a miniature dog, as other-worldly as a unicorn. After her came a young man dressed like a Western tourist. He was tall and very thin, with a pronounced Adam's apple, bulging bug eyes, and a mop of frizzy hair. Upon leaving the car, he turned and offered his hand to a young lady still inside. She wore white shorts, tennis shoes, and her hair up in a bun. In her hand she held two tennis rackets. Together the threesome entered the tennis stadium.

Fixated on the fortune-teller, Red-Haired Xuân barely noticed them. Instead, he prattled on about his alleged luck in love and continued to cross-examine the old man.

"What about money?! Will my fame bring me prosperity, or will I remain poor?"

"Not rich necessarily, but you'll be comfortable."

At this Xuân drifted off into his own thoughts, and his past flashed before him. When he was only nine, Xuân had lived with a distant paternal uncle whom the whole family praised for consenting magnanimously to take the boy in as his household servant. It was not long, however, before the uncle brutally beat Xuân and threw him out of the house. It seems that the boy had hollowed out a small hole in the washroom wall in order to spy on his uncle's wife while she bathed. From that day onward Xuân lived on the streets, subsisting initially on a diet of wild plums and minnows that he caught in the Restored Sword Lake. He sold roasted peanuts and newspapers on streetcorners, ran errands for a theater troupe, and hawked Tiger Balm aboard the trains. Moving from unskilled job to unskilled job, Xuân spent so much time outdoors that the sun dyed his hair a streaky red, as red as the hair of a Westerner. Lacking a formal education, he grew in street smarts and experience. Finally, he secured a job as a ball boy at the tennis stadium. There he was well treated, and his natural skill with a racket made him a favorite among the French and Vietnamese club members. His game improved, and he dreamed of one day becoming as famous as superstars like Chim or Giao, if only fate would dispatch a talent scout to discover his genius.[6] Now, however, he accepted his lot as a simple ball boy. Although the job was a lowly one, it held out a shred of hope for future advancement. He saw no future in old-fashioned professions such as peanut vending, fruit picking, fishing, or running errands for actors. His participation in the Sporting Movement . . . the Popular Movement . . . made him feel strangely proud and self-important.[7]

"Look at my face, old man. Do you see success or what?"

The fortune-teller examined Xuân's red-streaked hair, his receding forehead, his oversized jaw, his long flute of an upper lip, and his comically thick ears.

"Looks good. Your future looks very good, indeed. It's just too bad that your hair is no longer black."

"Damn it! That's what I get for not having a hat!"

Suddenly a little boy ran out of the tennis stadium, calling his name.

"Hey Xuân! Where are you!? She's here! She needs a partner! Are you coming or what!?"

"She's here?" Red-Haired Xuân repeated quizzically.

"Yes! It's that bitch, Miss Civilization—the one with the bean pole husband. And the other bitch, Mrs. Deputy Customs Officer, is here as well. She wants to play, too!"

Xuân stood up and barked at the fortune-teller: "Write it down for me, old man. I'll pick it up this afternoon or tomorrow. I've paid already, don't forget. Time for a little *ken co ban*[8] with the lovely lady. Just another notch in my belt!"

---

6. Popular Vietnamese tennis stars during the interwar era.

7. This is a reference to the political movement connected with the Front Populaire, which assumed power in France in 1936.

8. *Quelques balles* (some balls).

As he dashed toward the stadium, Xuân flashed Miss Sugar Cane a flirty smile.

"*O Voa!*[9] Till tomorrow!"

He entered the stadium and found three players waiting for him at the far-right court . . .

"Good afternoon, Grandmother. Good afternoon, Sir. Good afternoon, Madame."

Mr. and Mrs. Civilization nodded their heads in acknowledgment, but Mrs. Deputy Customs Officer turned away in disgust. The younger woman grinned knowingly at her husband.

"My aunt does not approve of such formal language," he said sternly to Xuân.

"You stupid ass!" Mrs. Deputy Customs Officer chimed in bitterly. "Who are you calling Grandmother? I'm no older than your mother. Do I look old enough to have delivered your mother? Why, I bet your mother is nothing more than a—"

"Yes, yes, Madame. I was mistaken. Please forgive me."

As the anger of this genuine *Me Tây*[10] began to dissipate, Xuân grabbed his racket and took to the court. Bop! Bop! The ball flew back and forth . . . Fixated on the creamy whiteness of Miss Civilization's thighs, Xuân failed to return several of her serves, thus creating the impression that her game had improved.

Still angry from the earlier insult, Mrs. Deputy Customs Officer gritted her teeth. "The Annamese are so stupid."

"Just ignore it Auntie," responded Mr. Civilization.

"I must play sports. Otherwise, I'll get old."

"I totally agree. But do you really feel this way, Auntie? Do you really like sports? If so, it is a great victory for sports! A harbinger of progress for Vietnam! And a sign of prosperity for our race!"

He spoke with an enthusiasm characteristic of numerous skinny and sickly men who celebrate the merits of sports without ever actually playing them. In the same vein he displayed a contempt for foreign diplomas that was common among Vietnamese students who had returned from six or seven years in France without ever actually earning one. In France he had grown close, so he claimed, to numerous well-known authors and statesmen—vice ministers

---

9. *Au revoir* (good bye).
10. Slang term meaning "wife of a Westerner."

and prime ministers—some so famous that their names had appeared in the Vietnamese press. When he returned home, the Security Police ordered two agents to follow him around. After three long months they concluded that his only secret activity involved furtively smoking Camel cigarettes. Eventually, he married a rich wife and adopted the surname Văn Minh, meaning "civilization"—a fact suspiciously noted by the Security Office. Through intensified surveillance they discovered that he had added his wife's surname, Văn (literature), to his own name, Minh (light), hence creating the new name. He saw the placement of his wife's name before his own as a simple act of gallantry and not, as others had surmised, as a sign of protest against patriarchy or an attempt to spearhead some sort of national or international reform movement. In fact, it signified nothing at all.

Since people now referred to him as Mr. Civilization, he felt compelled to support the ongoing campaign for Europeanization. To him this seemed a logical project, given the meaning of his new name. Soon thereafter, he overheard that universal truth—*a healthy soul demands a healthy body*—and thus he became a passionate proponent of sports, targeting his wife first and then the world at large. Unfortunately, his participation in the Europeanization campaign plunged him into such deep contemplation that he had precious little time for sports or for any exercise at all.

Mrs. Deputy Customs Officer's background is equally instructive. As a teenager, she had been raped by a Western soldier while journeying outside of her village to attend an Armistice Day festival. The soldier followed this unlawful rape with years of lawful rape—he married her, in other words. Afterwards, the soldier rose to the post of deputy customs officer and died ten years later. His death was not only a function of his fidelity to the state but of his unswerving fidelity to his wife—she literally screwed him to death. Almost immediately, she remarried a young official (this one of domestic vintage) who passed away under similar circumstances two years later. Because she had no known affairs, the tongues of poisonous snakes spread rumors that her poor husband had died of exhaustion while tending to her erotic flame—a flame fanned incessantly by her attentive admirers. It was her marital fidelity, in other words, that drove her poor husband to his death.

Two French girls and a young Vietnamese man appeared courtside, and Xuân chivalrously offered up his racket. When one of the French girls entered the changing room, Red-Haired Xuân abruptly disappeared.

The court buzzed with greetings and small talk. Balls flew back and forth like bats chasing mosquitoes through the air.

Moments later, a Frenchman emerged from behind the changing room, pulling Red-Haired Xuân by the hair. A small crowd gathered around as the Frenchman cursed Xuân and slapped him about the face and head. Xuân, it seems, had been up to his old tricks: spying on the French girl as she changed out of her skirt and into her tennis shorts. The Tennis Association fired him on the spot, refusing to forward him the remainder of his monthly salary.

Watching the scene unfold, Mrs. Deputy Customs Officer thought to herself that the people of Vietnam were not just stupid but pathetic as well. Sighing deeply, she said to her nephew: "Who has never made a mistake in their youth? We must forgive the foibles of the young. Poor guy. It's heartless for them to fire him like that!"

Chapter 2

Unlucky Stars: *Quan Phù* and *Thái Tuế*

◆

Alas for Our People! Civilization Ruined!

◆

Police and Police Fines

In the police station an officer escorted Red-Haired Xuân and the old fortune-teller across an empty courtyard and over to the door of a small ward. He turned the lock and motioned for them to enter.

"After you, Gentlemen," he said sarcastically.

Inside was a beggar together with his wife and child, a vagabond, and a female peddler with two baskets of stale noodles and rancid barbecue pork. The peddler sat against the wall, deep in thought, between her two baskets. The vagabond slept on the floor, snoring like a buzz saw. The beggar's wife and child huddled together, lovingly picking at each other's body lice. The door slammed shut, the lock clicked, and the patter of police boots faded into the distance . . . A dim light illuminated the room. Breathing heavily, the fortune-teller placed his mat and umbrella on the floor and sat down. Only Red-Haired Xuân remained standing. He scratched his sides and haughtily surveyed the room and its inhabitants.

"Police station, my ass!" he exclaimed, pursing his lips. "This jail's a snot hole. It's shameful!"

"I'm not shameful!" exclaimed the fortune-teller.

"No one's speaking to you, old man!" Xuân corrected him. "I'm talking about our government!"

The police station disgusted him. It was a small branch office for the city's newly created Eighteenth Precinct. Its seven officers included a French captain, a Vietnamese interpreter, an office manager, and four patrolmen. The sixteen streets under its jurisdiction were located in a French neighborhood that was so peaceful and secure that violations of the law were as rare as winning lottery tickets. So often did the four patrolmen speed without stopping through the sixteen streets that they grew to be talented cyclists. One had recently won the Tour de Hanoi–Hải Phòng. Others had placed third and fourth in the Tour de Hanoi–Sơn Tây, the Tour de Hanoi–Bắc Ninh, and the Tour de Hanoi–Hanoi. On those rare occasions when a peddler, a household servant, a cook, a rickshaw coolie, or a beggar did break a law—typically by pissing in the gutters or fighting in the streets—the patrolmen were never around. Since two were needed at all times to staff the station, there were only two left over to patrol all sixteen streets, and patrolling had become little more than training for bicycle races.

In response to the economic crisis and mounting budget deficit, the Financial and Economic Congress of Indochina ordered the various police headquarters in the city to collect a minimum of 40,000 piasters in fines; this station owed 5,000 piasters. The figure worried the French captain. He knew that only the lowliest Annamese—servants, cooks, rickshaw coolies, and street singers—were ticketed in his precinct. How could the station collect 5,000 piasters from such a pathetic collectivity? After mulling the problem over for several days, he came up with a brilliant plan. The next day all employees of the station were ordered to move their families to the sixteen streets. Over the next several weeks the French captain was fined for letting his dog run in the street. His wife was fined for lax management of her servant's house sweeping. Fines were also collected from the interpreter, the office manager, the four patrolmen, the errand boy, and the gardener. Their crimes included relieving themselves outside, cycling without a light, quarreling in public, poor household hygiene, etc. . . . They fined one another with a vengeance.

As the French captain was busy typing up some paperwork, a patrolman entered the office and reported a burglary at a nearby French residence. It had occurred the previous night but was only recently detected. The news annoyed the captain.

"Burglaries must be investigated at court," he said in French. "That means no fine for us."

43

Nevertheless, he left for the crime scene with the interpreter, leaving the office manager in charge of the station.

The office manager yawned like a merchant in the midst of a recession.

"Hey, Officer Min đơ!"[1] he called out glumly. "Is this pathetic or what?"

Officer Min đơ nodded gravely like a drunk and despondent Confucian scholar.

"Very pathetic! It's so pathetic it kills me!"

"We're being fined to death!" the office manager blurted out.

"It's unbearable!"

"I know the public budget is short of money and everything, but . . ."

"Our sixteen streets need more Annamese."

"Don't you miss the old days, say, ten years ago?"

"Very much so! Ten years ago our people were still stupid."

"Everyone is so civilized nowadays! It's a damn shame! The streets used to be filled with depraved, uncouth men and women— people who'd spit and piss wherever they pleased, people who'd beat each other up in public. Remember the days when four people rode together on a single bicycle!? Remember when people used to curse each other in public and smack their neighbors around? Houses were filthy with toilet water; dogs ran wild in the streets. Bicycles without headlights were everywhere. Now everything has changed. Alas, the good old days of our parents are gone forever!"

"Even rickshaw coolies obey the law, nowadays! They never forget their lights! They never stop in the middle of the road! No one even curses anyone's ancestors anymore! The old order has broken down completely! Kids today don't even know how to talk dirty! They're all so prim and proper. They don't climb trees; they don't play football in the middle of the road; they don't do anything!"

"It's the newspapers. That's the problem!"

"Exactly. The newspapers have civilized everyone. There's no one left to fine."

"Except us!"

"It's not right! It's inexcusable! We're the police, for Heaven's sake!"

1. *Mille deux* (1,002).

"I'm an officer manager! That's even worse, damn it! If not for the occasional bicycle race, my life would be an utter failure!"

"Can you imagine if our pictures did not appear, from time to time, on the front of the sports pages!?"

"Are you racing in the Tour de Hanoi–Hà Đông next Sunday?"

"Of course I am! After patrolling our sixteen streets four times a day without stopping to write a single ticket . . . I've never been in better shape. It would be a waste not to compete! But we've got to stop ticketing each other's families. Five thousand piasters! It's just not fair."

The office manager stood up and wagged his finger at Patrolman Min đơ.

"You cannot disobey an order, officer! Look at the wife of the French captain. We fined her twenty piasters last month, and she didn't utter a peep."

"If that's the case, then I must divorce my wife!"

"Oh no! Why so?"

"I told her not to keep the house so clean and to let the toilet clog up from time to time. I ordered her to let the children throw litter in the street—anything so that Patrolman Min toa[2] could ticket her, which would then allow me to ticket his wife in return. But the kids are as well behaved as little Buddhas, and the woman keeps the house spotless. What a witch!"

The office manager saw that he had struck a nerve and tried to change the subject. He ordered Min đơ to fetch the defendants from the jail for questioning.

As Officer Min đơ opened the door to the ward, the fortune-teller was scolding Red-Haired Xuân.

"See! That's what you get for being such a troublemaker. You get arrested! For me it makes no difference because this month my stars—Quan Phù and Thái Tuế—are unlucky anyway. They have foretold that, sooner or later during the month, I will be spending some time in court. For me to be arrested for something minor like this is not so bad!"

"I don't give a damn either, you old coot! Not to brag, but I've been arrested at least fifteen times already."

"Beating an old man is a violent offense. You could go to prison!"

---

2. *Mille trois* (1,003).

"Last time they took me to the Central Police Station! Now there's a real station. Half a dozen pistol-packing French officers with huge mustaches and chests covered with medals! Hundreds of policemen with white truncheons and huge chains. The ward has an iron bar like a tiger cage and holds hundreds of people, not to mention thousands of flies and mosquitoes! This jail is just a tiny snot hole. It barely holds a dozen people . . . It's a disgrace!"

"Let's go! Let's go!" Min đơ shouted. "It's time for interrogations. Shut your mouths and hurry up!"

Everyone stood up except the vagabond, who was snoring thunderously. Officer Min đơ gave him a kick.

"Let me sleep!" he moaned.

"Are you getting up, or do I have to drag you by the neck?"

"Getting up, Sir!" he said sulkily.

"Move on out!"

"First, they interrupt my sleep to bring me to jail, and now they wake me up again to release me. What a pain!"

The prisoners filed out of the cell, through the courtyard, and into the front office.

Because Red-Haired Xuân was respectably dressed in French-style shorts, tennis shoes, and a sleeveless undershirt, the office manager turned to him first.

"What's this guy's crime!?"

"He hit me, Your Honor," the fortune-teller blurted out.

"I did not," Xuân protested. "I was just wringing his neck!"

"He hit me hard two times, then he tried to strangle me . . ."

"I never hit him, and there wasn't enough time to strangle him. He's such a crybaby . . ."

The manager rapped his fist on the table.

"Quiet! Quiet! I'm asking the questions here! I'll get to the bottom of this! You! Why did you hit him?"

"He ripped me off, Sir. I gave him one *hào* for a fortune reading, but his predictions were completely wrong, and he refused to give me a refund. I only want my money back. I didn't mean to hit him."

The manager turned to the fortune-teller. "Did you read his fortune? Did you receive one *hào*?"

"I gave him a discount, Your Honor. One *hào* is a bargain. All my predictions were accurate, and yet he still wants his money back."

"Not true, Your Honor! He said my future looked bright, and the next thing I knew I lost my job!"

The manager frowned at the fortune-teller. "You dare to keep his money after a lousy prediction like that!?"

"The future is still in the future, Your Honor. It has yet to arrive. I have studied the art of fortune-telling for ten years, and my predictions are rarely off the mark. And I am never completely wrong! Please do not judge my skills, Your Honor, until you have had the chance to sample them yourself."

The manager frowned at Red-Haired Xuân. "That sounds reasonable to me!"

"Take your own facial features for example, Your Honor," the fortune-teller continued. "The fame and fortune quadrant looks very good. You are a real fire breather. The length of your eyebrows indicates that you have many brothers, and your flabby earlobes signify great wealth in the future!"

The manager frowned at Red-Haired Xuân one more time. "This fortune-teller has real talent. *A lê!*[3] You committed the crime of hitting an old person! You are fined one *đồng* and eight *hào!* Release the fortune-teller immediately! And, you, let me see your identity card!"

Out on the street a car pulled up in front of the station. Mrs. Deputy Customs Officer entered the front office and smiled at the officers, who smiled back like merchants greeting a rich customer. Because Mrs. Deputy Customs Officer often let her dog loose, she had been ticketed at least once on each of the precinct's sixteen streets. To the police, in other words, she was like a regular customer of a failing business.

"What can we do for you, Madame?"

"I am here to pay a fine for this servant of mine," she replied, pointing at Xuân. "Please release him."

The manager rubbed his hands together. "First the fine, if you please, Madame."

"How much?"

"One *đồng* and eight *hào.*"

Red-Haired Xuân looked on in amazement as Officer Min đơ wrote up a receipt.

---

3. *Allez!* (Go!).

47

"Great Madame," he said respectfully. "Why are you taking such pity on me?"

"You will know soon enough . . . when I get you home! You have a job already."

"See!?" the fortune-teller exclaimed. "Do you still say that I am wrong!"

"I take it back," Xuân replied. "You are indeed a living saint! My deepest apologies to you, Sir!"

"What did you say?" asked Mrs. Deputy Customs Officer.

"Madame, this fortune-teller has great powers!"

"Is that so? Please come to my house and read my fortune! My car will take you!"

She handed over the money and grabbed the receipt. After fetching his belongings from the cell, the fortune-teller followed Xuân and Mrs. Deputy Customs Officer into her car. The office manager saw them off at the gate. Forgetting momentarily that he was at the police station and not the French bakery owned by his wife, he called out after the car, "Thank you so much! Please come again!"

Chapter 3

Son of Heaven, Son of Buddha

☙

The Reincarnation of the Famous
Soothsayer *Quỷ Cốc Tử*

☙

A Suspicious Case

The car honked like the grunt of a wild boar. Moments later a man-servant appeared, opened both wings of the iron gate, and waved the car into the courtyard. An electric streetlight overhanging the outer wall of the compound illuminated a huge Western-style villa surrounded by a massive garden of willows, hibiscus, cacti, *spica* plants, terra cotta pillars, and rows upon rows of strange flowers. The garden excited Xuân. He sensed the beginning of a new chapter of his life. The fortune-teller smirked and elbowed Xuân in the ribs as if to remind him that he had recently predicted as much. Sitting beside the placid chauffeur, Xuân dared not respond.

The car pulled up in front of a twelve-step cement stairway that led to the front door of the house. The driver got out of the car and opened the back door. Mrs. Deputy Customs Officer stepped out, carrying a dog, a Japanese umbrella, and a leather purse. She was followed by the old fortune-teller with his box, his umbrella, and his straw mat. Xuân exited last, and the car returned to the garage. A woman, dressed as a servant, scampered down the steps to fetch the luggage for her mistress.

"And where is the little master? What is he doing?" asked Mrs. Deputy Customs Officer.

"Excuse me, Mistress. He's taking a bath."

"A bath? Has he eaten?"

Without waiting for an answer, she turned back to address Miss Three. "Miss Three! Why do you bathe him out here in the yard? Why do you let him expose himself outside?"

"That's what he wanted. As you know, the little master cries if he does not get what he wants."

In a giant brass tub sat an obese little boy with the face of a half-wit. Although over a meter in height, he splashed about in the water like a three-year-old child. The ground around the tub was littered with toys: a stuffed dog, a doll, a car, a plane, a trumpet . . . Mrs. Deputy Customs Officer put down her dog.

"Taking a bath, my sweet? What a good boy! Did anyone beat you while mother was out? Lulu! Up! Up!"

Mrs. Deputy Customs Officer whistled twice. The dog sat up unsteadily on his two hind legs and held out his front paws. He wagged his tongue to greet the little boy in the bath. Slapping at the water rhythmically with both hands, the boy looked at the dog and frowned.

"No way!" he screamed.

"Here, here . . . Mother apologizes. Let Mother give you a kiss."

"No way!"

Mrs. Deputy Customs Officer hesitated for a moment. "Go ahead and take your bath. But come in afterwards and eat with Mother, okay?"

"No way!"

"All right, as you wish. But if you love Mother, at least give her a kiss."

Stark naked, the little boy stood up in the bath and kissed his mother. But, good God! The little master was certainly not little anymore! The scene possessed a certain bizarre fascination for the onlookers; it was at least as interesting as a pornographic photo. As the "uncouth" servants frequently observed, the boy's "equipment" was already in working order.

"That boy is the Son of Heaven, the Son of Buddha," explained Mrs. Deputy Customs Officer.

The fortune-teller understood this to mean that the boy had been born only after his mother had prayed in dozens of pagodas. Xuân, on the other hand, was flabbergasted. As soon as Mrs. Deputy Customs Officer entered the house, the little master began to scream and sob.

"Where's Miss Three?" Mrs. Deputy Customs Officer shouted from within the house.

The boy continued to yell.

"Little Master wants to go in! Little Master wants in!"

"Miss Three! Hurry up!" urged Mrs. Deputy Customs Officer. "Dry off the Little Master and bring him inside."

Mrs. Three picked the child up and carried him into the house, piggyback style. The enormous little master gyrated up and down as if riding a horse.

"Gitty-up! Gitty-up! Gitty-up!"

Xuân was so disgusted he could hardly bear it.

"God-damned brat," he murmured to himself.

Xuân and the fortune-teller entered the living room. Mrs. Deputy Customs Officer pointed them toward the sofa. "Sit here and wait for me."

She left into the next room.

While they waited, the gigantic little boy appeared at the door wearing a shirt but no pants. He poked his head in and out of the door and giggled to himself like an imbecile. His silk shirt, the color of chicken fat, displayed large red insignias on both sides that were supposed to ward off evil spirits. Around his neck was a thick gold choker on which hung a small pendant and a huge gold medallion.

The plaintive wail of Miss Three echoed from the other room: "Master Blessing! Master Blessing! Please put on your pants!"

"No way!"

"Put on your pants, or the guests will laugh at you."

"Make them play with me!"

"Yes, yes . . . But put your pants on first."

"No way."

"That kid really is a gift from heaven!" said the fortune-teller furtively.

Xuân nodded in agreement.

"But it's strange," the fortune-teller continued. "The mistress seems like a Frenchman's wife."

"Right on," Xuân whispered, covering his mouth with his hand.

"So, why does her 'gift from heaven' look so Annamese?"

Before Xuân could respond, he heard the voice of Mrs. Deputy Customs Officer.

"My boy! My beloved boy! Put on your clothes. Be a good boy . . ."

Mrs. Deputy Customs Officer entered the living room. She had taken off her gown, brassiere, and head-dress and had put on an utterly transparent silk shirt and paper-thin pants. This made her seem like a passionate adherent of nudism, while it made Xuân feel dirty and uncouth. The old fortune-teller stood up respectfully.

"Do you tell fortunes by physiognomy or by horoscope?" she asked.

"I do both, Great Madame."

"Which way is more accurate?"

"Horoscope."

"Fine. Do mine."

"When is your date of birth, Great Madame?"

"I'm not sure. I don't remember exactly."

"In that case I will do your physiognomy. But I'm afraid it won't be as detailed as a horoscope."

"That's fine. Go ahead."

"Great Madame's physiognomy is quite encouraging. Of the twelve sectors of your face, only one is of any concern—the one that relates to your husband. You see, Great Madame, your cheekbones are rather high."

Mrs. Deputy Customs Officer frowned.

"What do you mean? What's wrong with my husbands? The deputy customs officer was always very good to me. And so was the senior clerk. He was very kindhearted. Right before the senior clerk died, he said that he still loved me. How many people are so beloved by their husbands?"

"Yes, Great Madame. But, according to ancient tradition, multiple husbands must be interpreted as an inauspicious sign."

"Yes, you are right. But, according to modern traditions, one can enjoy as many husbands as one likes, as long as they are kind. Your physiognomic skill is great."

"Your character, Great Madame, is very humane. You display great compassion for other people."

"Your physiognomic skill is truly great."

"Your financial sector looks good. Your land sector looks even better. The sector regarding your ancestor's tombs is very positive as well."

"What about the sector relating to my children?"

"Also good. But a little sparse."

Mrs. Deputy Customs Officer frowned. "Why so? I have two children. My Jannette is in high school. She will graduate soon. And little Master Blessing is growing very fast. In three months he will be eleven. Why do you say 'sparse' when I have two children?"

"Great Madame, there is an old saying: 'One son counts, ten girls don't.' According to the old teachings, daughters are worthless, no matter how abundant. Hence, a single son must be considered rather sparse."

"I see. One son is sparse."

"Great Madame. Do you plan to remarry?"

"Certainly not! I'm determined . . . I pledge on the souls of my deputy customs officer and my senior clerk to remain a widow. Even though I'm still very young . . . I vow to stay single to raise my children."

"It is as I said, Great Madame. The sector regarding your children is a little sparse."

"Your physiognomic skill is great. What about the fate of little Master Blessing? Buddhas from the Perfume Pagoda have blessed me with his presence for over ten years already. I only worry that—"

"Great Madame. That sector is the best. I predict a life of great leisure. He will enjoy wealth, high rank, security, and good health."

Mrs. Deputy Customs Officer looked down respectfully and said in a low voice, "I . . . I only worry that, as a mere earthly being, I do not know how to please him and he will decide to return to the heavens from where he came."

"Not to worry! Not to worry! Just look at his physiognomy! He will live a long life. And Great Madame will have even greater wealth thanks to him."

"Great! Great! Your physiognomic skill is exceptional, truly wonderful!"

"Great Madame. If you tell me your exact time of birth, I can construct a horoscope chart that will show what will happen to you every year, every month, and every day . . ."

"Is that so?"

"Yes, Great Madame. A horoscope chart is much more accurate than physiognomy."

"Fine. You should leave, as it will soon be dark. Please come back in a day or two and do a horoscope for me! Where is Miss Three? Give him one *đồng* for rickshaw fare. Be sure to come back for that horoscope reading."

"Yes, yes. Great Madame, I'll be back in a day or two."

The old fortune-teller picked up his umbrella, straw mat, and box and left.

Mrs. Deputy Customs Officer turned to Xuân: "You! Do you know what I did for you?"

The question caught Xuân off guard; he felt confused and a little frightened.

"Great Madame, without your help, I would still be in jail."

"Yes. You should be grateful."

"Great Madame, your child will never forget that favor."

"Do not call yourself 'child' to me! I am a civilized woman. I do not discriminate. I do not distinguish between the rich and the poor . . ."

"Yes, Madame."

"Are your parents still alive?"

"Madame, I lost my parents when I was small."

"Poor you! Do you have a wife? children?"

"Not yet, Madame."

"That's great! Uh . . . I mean that's a real shame! Anyway, these are difficult times; you should not get married too early. Do you know why I called you here?"

"Not yet, Madame. I'm waiting to serve you."

"I am a humane woman. I feel great compassion. And you deserve my compassion. You were working and suddenly lost your job. It must be terrible for you. Why were you acting so silly in that changing room? I know that young people are often frisky, but you must first determine whether the other person agrees or not. Then . . . See?"

"I don't know what happened, Madame," Xuân said innocently. "Suddenly they beat me, they fired me, they oppressed me . . ."

"Now, now. There's no need to deny what you did!"

"Deny what . . . Madame?"

"So, why did they fire you?"

"I really don't know. As I was preparing cotton towels for the club members, that Western man came in, dragged me out of the dressing room, beat me, and scolded me."

"You weren't doing anything . . . ?"

Xuân contrived the most innocent expression he could muster. "I was just plugging a hole in the changing room of the club."

"So, why didn't you protest when that Western fellow accused you of such a crime?"

Xuân's face turned red. "Oh Madame!" he stammered. "I don't even know what he accused me of. I don't understand French . . ."

Mrs. Deputy Customs Officer stood dumbfounded and swallowed her disappointment.

She recalled her embarrassments and mistakes in the past. Ever since she had been raped, those rare and semiconscious sensations—sensations that were strange and very difficult to describe—continued to cling to her as a shadow clings to a body. Gradually, they had become her obsession. She desired to be ravished again, but the opportunity never arose. Instead, she had been forced to ravish her husbands. By reading the novel *The Tearful History of Kim Anh*, she learned of the existence of a provincial monk who claimed to be a Buddha who could guarantee children for women who prayed at his pagoda. After searching for and eventually finding the pagoda, she was embarrassed to discover that the story was a hoax. Although the ministrations of the monk did not pan out, she eventually received a son from her second husband, Mr. Senior Clerk.

But now.

Examining Xuân's honest face, she came to the depressing realization that he had probably been falsely accused. Just as her sadness began turning to anger, an idea suddenly popped into her head.

"Go upstairs and wait for me to take my bath. Afterwards, I will tell you why I asked you here."

Xuân obeyed . . . He followed her upstairs and into another guest room.

"Sit here and wait for me. Here, take a look at this *an bum*."[1]

She left into the bathroom a few steps away from where Xuân sat.

---

1. Album.

She undressed, put on a rubber bathing cap to cover her hair, and turned on the water. Water cascaded down from the iron shower-head. As she washed, she made conspicuously loud slapping noises on her stomach and thighs. Getting no response, she knelt down and peered through the keyhole of the bathroom door. Xuân was looking attentively at the pictures in the album. He remained in his seat.

"Not again!" she thought to herself.

She finished bathing and opened the door. "Enough already. You can go. I plan to hire you tomorrow. Tomorrow, go to the Europeanization Tailor Shop and ask for Mrs. Civilization. I will put in a word for you. You will not be jobless any longer."

"Please . . ."

"Enough! You are not very smart! Go away! Tomorrow you will see. Remember, the Europeanization Tailor Shop . . . for women."

Red-Haired Xuân left, his heart full of hope. He was oblivious to the fact that she momentarily despised him, just as she despised all men who were truly moral.

Chapter 4

The Anger of *Hoạn Thư*[1]
—
Art for Life's Sake
—
The Products of Europeanization

Following the instructions he had received from Mrs. Deputy Customs Officer, Red-Haired Xuân arrived in front of a modern-looking tailor shop for women at precisely eight the next morning. He dared not enter immediately, however, for he could not be sure if this was, in fact, the Europeanization Tailor Shop of Mrs. Civilization. Red-Haired Xuân's limited education had endowed him with the capacity to make out a laundry list but not to understand the ultramodern and largely illegible lettering favored by today's advertising designers. As Xuân looked on, workers were putting up a new storefront sign. Five bizarre-looking pieces of newly painted red wood lay drying on the pavement. One worker had propped a ladder up against the wall. A younger man, whose rolled-up shirtsleeves indicated that he meant business, barked out orders and issued occasional rebukes. The tailor shop was remarkably swank. Three wooden *ma nơ canh*[2] imported from Europe stood poised behind its large plate-glass window. Although they had been made to resemble beautiful European women, the shop owner had skillfully arranged turbans and strands of black hair on their heads so as to make them

---

1. Character from Nguyễn Du's celebrated verse narrative *Kim Vân Kiều*, renowned for her jealousy.
2. Mannequins.

look more Vietnamese. Each mannequin displayed a different article of clothing. One sported a swallow-tailed coat, the kind that girls and young women often wear to go out. Another wore a swimming suit, the kind that girls and young women wear on the beach in order to display the art of their bodies. A third wore lingerie, the kind worn by powerful women so as to remind their husbands and lovers not to forget their most sacred of masculine duties.

Xuân inched toward the five wooden letters on the pavement. Try as he might, he was unable to make out the specific letter that each was supposed to symbolize. There was a round one with a hole in the middle and a strange square one with two round holes in the middle. Even more bizarre were three triangle-shaped ones with holes in the middle! Ever since he was six, Red-Haired Xuân's coarse mind knew that a triangular shape with a hole in the middle could only signify one thing—one very dirty thing. He smiled to himself.

The young man with the rolled-up sleeves began shouting at his workers. "No! No! This one goes first! The triangle, damn it!"

"What is a triangle?" asked the worker, confusedly.

The young man scolded him again. "A triangle . . . with a hole, damn it! And the triangular shape here is supposed to be the letter *A*."

"But, Sir," the worker protested, "you just said that the triangular shape is the letter *U*."

"You idiot! The right-side up triangle is a *U*. The upside-down one is an *A*. What kind of craftsman are you? Don't you know anything about art? Nail the upside-down triangle first, then put the right-side-up one after it. That's *A* followed by *U*—giving us *ÂU*—Europe in other words. Then put up the square piece with the two holes—that's an *H*. Then the round piece with a hole in the middle—that's an *O*. Then another upside-down triangle—I mean another *A*. That spells *HOÁ*-ization. Together, it all means Europeanization! Get it? You guys are dumber than pigs!"

Despite the insult, Xuân was happy to have found the shop.

"Screw those god-damned letters!" he murmured to himself.

A moment later a young man appeared wearing a European hiking outfit. He approached the young man overseeing the design of the storefront sign. They shook hands and greeted each other noisily in French.

"My God! The Vietnamese common people are so backward, artistically speaking."

"Yes, yes, it's simply a waste of breath to talk about art with the common people."

"Of course, but remember that you are a journalist. Your duty is to help enhance the knowledge of the common people so that one day they too may understand art. I, on the other hand, am an artist. I am much too busy devoting myself to art to explain my work to them."

"Yes, but your influence is already quite widespread, even among ordinary folk."

"Still not enough. There is much work to be done. Ours are a lazy people. They do not want to think deeply; they rarely try to comprehend the vast, complicated problems that those of us in the fine arts must confront. Of course, the more difficult a work of art is to understand, the more valuable it is. For example, in Italy and in Germany, I hear, those painters whose works are completely incomprehensible are worshiped as saints. When the dictators Hitler and Mussolini took power, they were so jealous of these artists that they threw them in jail. I only pray that someday our artists will be good enough to be thrown in jail as well!"

"Indeed!"

"Due to the low level of our society, we artists must take responsibility for the reform of women's fashions—by far the easiest genre of fine arts to understand. Only when our society learns to enjoy the beauty of . . . women's thighs, will it be able to appreciate the value of nude paintings and thus appreciate fine art at the highest level."

"Quite right!"

"How do you like these ultramodern letters? They are my latest creation! Aren't they unusual? The fact that the most common people cannot understand this style of lettering only confirms its sophistication. Someday I hope to craft letters that are so very, very modern that even intellectuals cannot read them. What a victory for art!"

While eavesdropping on this conversation, Xuân caught a glimpse of Mrs. Civilization through the storefront window. He gingerly entered the shop. The two young men followed him inside, still engrossed in conversation.

"Good morning, Madame," Xuân said politely.

Mrs. Civilization nodded to Xuân and shook hands with the other two. "Please sit down, Monsieurs. To what do we owe this visit?" she asked the journalist. "Are subscriptions up or down these days?"

"I've come for an important reason. Our sales are up to fifty copies . . ."

She cut him off briskly and turned to Xuân.

"And what about you? What can I do for you?"

Xuân blushed and rubbed his hands together.

"If you please . . . please . . . Yesterday, the great Madame Deputy Customs Officer . . ."

Mrs. Civilization interrupted him.

"Quiet! You must refer to her as Madame Senior Clerk; otherwise, she will be annoyed."

"Yes, Ma'am! Madame Senior Clerk told me to come here . . . she said . . . to meet you . . ."

"Fine. Wait here for a moment."

Mrs. Civilization gestured to the journalist to enter the salon inside the shop. Xuân sat down on an upholstered chair near the door. Despite his nervousness, he took advantage of the rare opportunity to admire those secret aspects of the gentler sex that only the Europeanization movement dares to display openly. It was truly a party for his eyes—provocative breasts cupped in brassieres of silk and lace, thighs cased in sheer silk stockings and all manner of slips and panties, each capable of provoking lust in men well into their seventies. Huge colorful rolls of solid and floral-patterned silk gave the shop an especially lively ambiance. There was also a dressing room covered on three sides by velvet drapes and another room in which male and female tailors worked, busy as bees, before a row of sewing machines.

A poorly made-up middle-aged woman appeared outside the glass window. She gazed inside for several minutes before entering the shop. The shop owner greeted her warmly.

"Can I help you, Madame? Would you like to buy clothes or perhaps have something made?"

The customer thought for a long while. "I want . . . a custommade modern outfit."

"Of course you do," Mrs. Civilization replied glibly. "Today we must all reform our wardrobes to keep up with fashion. The conventional trends in makeup, for example, tend to make people look older. We must replace them! As you know, Madame, one can no longer remain ignorant of the latest fads in beauty maintenance and hope to maintain family happiness. Nowadays, all young girls dress in a modern way—the competition is increasingly brutal."

The woman nodded and opened her eyes wide in agreement. "Yes! Yes! You are absolutely right! Young girls today dress even more provocatively than wives of Westerners in the past! So modern! So slutty! My god! They are so beautiful compared to me, and my husband is obsessed by them. What am I to do?"

Her voice rose to an almost hysterical pitch. Mrs. Civilization tried to calm her down. "Now, now! Don't get so worked up!"

"But my husband spends every night chasing after those modern sluts! What, for Heaven's sake, can I do?"

"The answer is simple, Madame. If you can't beat them, you must join them. You must try to dress just like them."

"Yes! Yes! I can dress like that too, of course! Who cares if people call me an old whore! It's all your doing anyway. It all starts with you tailors!"

Mrs. Civilization shrugged her shoulders.

"Madame, our society progresses according to the basic laws of evolution. During this deeply reformist era everything conservative will be eliminated! Since we opened this tailor shop, countless wives have saved their marriages, recaptured the love of their husbands, and reestablished the happiness of their families."

"In that case, Madame, I would like to order a custom-made outfit right away, the most modern possible! Only, please do not charge me too much!"

"Of course! I will be happy to suggest several new and different styles for you . . ."

Mrs. Civilization drew the attention of her customer to a row of mannequins. "See . . . here . . . The many innovative styles displayed in our shop were all designed by well-known art students. If you please, Madame, the sign under each mannequin explains the meaning of the outfit it displays. For example, this one is called 'Promise.' A girl may wear this outfit to reassure her boyfriend that she promises to show up for their appointment that evening. This one is called 'Win His Heart.' Men are like putty in the hands of girls who wear this outfit. And here, of course, we have 'Innocence.' This one is

'Puberty'—appropriate for teenage girls. Clothes in this section are for 'Commanders of Internal Affairs'—housewives, in other words. This one is called 'Women's Rights,' for wives whose husbands are afraid of them. This one, 'Resolute Faithfulness,' is for widows determined to honor their late husbands and remain unmarried. This one, 'Hesitation,' is for widows who are somewhat less determined. And here we have our newest model, finished several days ago. We have not named it formally yet, but we are planning to call it 'Conquest.' In this outfit you should be able to stoke the passions of any man, even your own husband!"

Conquest consisted of a transparent black blouse and pair of pants over a set of black panties and a black *coóc xê*[3]. It also exposed the arms, deep cleavage, thighs, and legs of the beautiful wooden woman that exhibited it. Mrs. Civilization stared at the outfit with a look of utter satisfaction.

The customer, however, appeared unconvinced. "To wear this outfit . . . well, it's just unsightly!"

At that moment the journalist and artist joined the conversation.

"It's very sightly indeed, Madame!" the journalist said. "If you wear this outfit, men will pursue you, just as they pursue innocent young girls!"

"Ah, Conquest!" the artist chimed in. "I chose the name, you know."

"But such clothing barely covers anything at all," the customer protested.

"Madame," the artist retorted, "the very concept of clothing has changed. We developed this particular style following the conceptual lead of famous European designers. Clothing should enhance and embellish one's natural beauty, not cover it up. Soon clothing will progress to that extreme, exquisite, perfect point where it will no longer cover up anything at all."

Mrs. Civilization peered uneasily at the doubtful expression on the face of her customer.

"It may seem too modern for you now, but just wait until the next time your husband plans to go on one of his evening outings. As soon as you put it on and stand before the mirror, your husband will desire no one but you."

---

3. Corset (bra).

"Yes! Yes!" the customer nodded. "Perhaps I ought to give that one a try."

"Madame, what is family happiness if not the happiness of husbands and wives? What else can be done when love begins to fade?"

"You're right! You're absolutely right!"

"We have designed new styles of undergarments for this same reason. Never mind what those old-fashioned moralists say about us. We do not simply *reform the outside.* A slip or a pair of panties from our shop may be thought of as a secret weapon in the fight to retain one's husband."

"Where are they? How can I order one?"

Mrs. Civilization turned around and gestured toward a glass case. She reached in and pulled out a pile of panties, brassieres, long slips, and mini-slips.

"I call this one 'Coquette.' And these are known as 'Wait-a-Minute' panties. This is the 'Happiness' slip. Here is what we call the 'Stop-Those-Hands' brassiere. Feel free to look them over. Only the Europeanization Shop cares so much about the satisfaction of the fair sex."

The female customer nodded her head vigorously. "Yes, I will do as you say! I will Europeanize myself and follow the ways of civilization! I vow to dress progressively! Call your tailors and show me the changing room!"

Mrs. Civilization pointed to the artist. "Here, Madame, is your tailor! He was originally a student at the Indochinese Fine Art College. Your beauty is now his responsibility!"

The artist bowed his head very low. "Please follow me, Madame. I am deeply honored to serve you."

They disappeared behind the velvet drapes of the changing room. Xuân remained in his chair. Mrs. Civilization turned to address the journalist.

"Monsieur, your newspaper cannot possibly propose to charge more for advertising. The cost is excessive already."

"You are wrong, Madame. Our newspaper has more and more readers everyday. Our prestige is constantly under attack by conservative forces—another clear benefit to you. More people are following the news than ever before."

"That is only natural, Monsieur. But, of course, it benefits your business much more than mine."

"No! It benefits you and your kind as well, maybe even more!"

"It is you who calls for renovation. Hence, you benefit most when people heed the call!"

"No! You benefit most!"

"So says you!"

"It's not true! Haven't you noticed the recent progressive evolution of our society? It's all over the daily papers! So many divorces! So many cases of adultery! Girls chasing boys, men getting bored with their wives, officials leaving their posts to pursue modern girls . . . It's great for your business. Newspapers clearly have a huge influence. New dancing halls are popping up everyday . . ."

At that moment Mrs. Deputy Customs Officer entered the shop. Red-Haired Xuân stood up. Mrs. Civilization left the journalist alone to contemplate the influence of his newspaper.

"My niece! My niece! . . ."

"Auntie . . . Over here . . . I need to ask you something."

Aunt and niece huddled together in the far corner of the room. As the journalist put on his hat and walked angrily out of the shop, he grasped one of life's basic truths: journalism is a wretched profession. Red-Haired Xuân continued to wait.

"Why did you send this guy here, Auntie?"

"I need you to hire him. I want to keep him around while they are building the tennis court at my house. We can use him for practice."

"But the court won't be finished for a while. Why hire him now and waste all that money?"

"You have a point. But he may starve if we don't do it now!"

She paused a moment and then whispered to her niece: "How about this . . . before the tennis court is finished, we could . . . in that way, we won't waste all that much. What do you think?"

Just like that, Red-Haired Xuân became a member of the movement for social reform.

Chapter 5

A Lesson in Progress for Red-Haired Xuân
●
Two Views about Family and Society
●
A Horned Husband

The clock struck twelve.

Mr. and Mrs. Civilization drove to a restaurant for lunch, accompanied by several modern-looking women and a handful of students recently returned from studies abroad. The tailors and seamstresses also went out to eat together. Out on the street cicadas hummed in the *sapindus* trees, disturbing the afternoon naps of high officials.

"What a god-damned drag," said Red-Haired Xuân to himself. He paced back and forth, trying to commit to memory the instructions he had received from his new boss.

"Before you help us to practice sports, we need you to assist in the Europeanization of society. Keep in mind that from this day forward you play an important part in the Movement for Social Reform. From now on your efforts will determine whether our society grows more civilized or degenerates into barbarity! Hence, you must work hard, take your responsibilities seriously, and try to understand the significance of what you are doing."

Seeing Xuân's blank reaction to the Master's convoluted advice, the Mistress tried to put it more simply.

"What he means is that, if you find yourself with free time, use this feather duster to tidy up the place. Start with the spools of silk and then do the clothes and the mannequins. Cleanliness is important. Do not let the doorway become dusty and full of litter."

"Yes, Ma'am."

"You must also learn the names of various products and fashions," added the designer, "so that you can make suggestions to customers regarding *gu!*"[1]

"Yes, Sir. But what is *gu?*"

The designer tapped his brow, searching for the right words. "It means . . . It means a certain liking or a taste," he stammered. "It is a specific concept about fine art."

"I still don't get it, Sir."

"Try to understand! In order to please the customers' ears, you must remember all the names. This is the duty of the *văng đơ.*[2] Every time someone buys a new modern outfit, our country will have another progressive person."

"Sir, do I also need to know the different kinds of silk—and how to match certain fabrics with certain kinds of ladies?"

The designer opened his eyes wide and stuck his finger in Xuân's face. "Of course not! That's too much to expect from the likes of you. Only French *tay ơ*[3] like me can be trusted to carry out such a sacred duty! This is my work! Mine! Here, come with me . . ."

The designer dragged Xuân over to a mannequin. "Sleeveless and neckless means Puberty! Say it aloud!"

Xuân repeated after him like a parrot cramming for an exam. "Sleeveless and neckless means Puberty! Sleeveless and neckless means Puberty!"

The designer nodded and directed Xuân to another mannequin. "Strapless, showing the top half of the breasts means Innocence! Repeat after me."

"Strapless, showing the top half of the breasts means Innocence! Strapless, showing the top half of the breasts means Innocence!"

Red-Haired Xuân repeated it again and again.

"Very good! If you learn these by heart, you should be able eventually to recognize the lettering on the signs. Soon you will know every style ever devised by the fine art of fashion design. From now

---

1. *Gôut* (taste).
2. *Vendeur* (salesperson).
3. *Tailleur* (tailor).

on the Europeanization Movement will hinge on your intelligent mind, so pay attention. This outfit, Resolute Faithfulness, is for widows determined not to remarry. Hence, neither the top nor the bottom is especially revealing; the collar is like a lotus leaf, draped over the bulging outlines of the breasts. With Hesitation, on the other hand, the collar is designed to cover one side of the breast and reveal the other. Can you read these labels?"

"Yes Sir, I know how to read the old-style lettering."

"Good. In that case I'll leave you to go over them by yourself."

"Don't forget to hang the Closed at Noon sign in front of the glass window," Mrs. Civilization added. "You will stay here and mind the shop. If anyone comes, greet them and try to remember what they ask for so you can tell me later."

With that, they left the shop.

The designer's comments confirmed to Red-Haired Xuân that he was no more than an errand boy in the Europeanization Movement for Social Reform. While this fact did not disturb him, he was miffed that no one remembered that errand boys need lunch and an afternoon rest like other people. He was starving, in fact. He had hoped to meet Mrs. Deputy Customs Officer, but she had driven away long ago with her beloved dog.

In the now quiet and empty shop he paced back and forth, murmuring to himself. "What a god-damned pain in the—!"

He began dusting off the mannequins. Like a child studying Chinese characters by heart, Xuân read each label several times out loud to himself.

"God-damn these clothes! What the hell is this one? Promise, huh? Tight waist, wide at the chest and ass . . . got it! Tight waist, wide chest and ass is Promise! Breasts, arms, and thighs exposed— Conquest! Breasts, arms, and thighs exposed—Conquest! Strapless, showing the top half of the breasts, is Innocence!"

Xuân dropped the feather duster and bent down to pick it up.

"Strapless, showing the top half of the breasts, is Innocence! Strapless . . . strapless . . . is Innocence!"

At that moment a young woman pushed open the door and entered the shop. She stared at Xuân in surprise. "Who are you?"

Red-Haired Xuân hid the feather duster behind his back. "Me? I am . . . I am . . . a member of the Europeanization Movement," he said solemnly.

"I see!"

"I am a social reformer . . . the future of our nation lies in my hands."

"Ah yes, very good!"

"What can I do for you, Miss? A pair of Wait-a-Minute panties perhaps?"

"I'm sorry, but I can't wait a minute. You see, I'm married already."

"Then what do you want, Madame?"

"I want my husband! I want reform! I want Europeanization! Do you know where my husband is?"

"Who is he, Madame?"

"Mr. ILL . . . !

"Who?"

"Mr. ILL!"

Red-Haired Xuân stood frozen in place, as wooden looking as the mannequins.

"Mr. . . . Mr. ILL?"

"Yes! Right. Where is he?"

"There is no Mr. ILL here!"

"But, there is. He is a tailor known as Mr. Indochinese Fine Arts. As a columnist for the women's newspapers, he uses the pen name Mr. ILL—it stands for 'I Love Ladies!' All social reformers know of him. Since when did you start to reform?"

"Ah, ah, yes, of course! He just stepped out . . ."

"I'll wait for him."

"Yes, please relax, Madame. As you wish."

"Please tell me what you think, Monsieur. Does my outfit seem at all modern to you?"

Red-Haired Xuân glanced at her simple *áo dài*. Her collar was not shaped like a lotus leaf. Her white pants were plain and unrevealing. Her unpretentious shoes were made of black velvet. Given his recent realization that the most modern clothes were the ones that looked the most absurd, her outfit seemed rather old-fashioned.

"Madame, you look honest and proper only. There appears to be little modern about you."

"Say it isn't so, Monsieur!"

Xuân nodded insistently.

"Very old-fashioned, in fact, not Europeanized at all! The outfit seems especially dated for the wife of Mr. ILL . . . Don't you know that your husband has designed many of the newest and most elegant styles? Innocence, Conquest, Hesitation, Wait-a-Minute, Coquette, Stop-Those-Hands . . ."

The woman ground her teeth together. "My husband oppresses me. I can't bear it any longer!"

"Madame, that is truly a roadblock on the road of evolution! Your only course of action is to order the outfit known as Women's Rights. It is guaranteed to strike fear into the heart of your husband . . . Civilization has said as much!"

"You are a highly educated man. You speak as eloquently as French literature! Please help me get through this Europeanization Movement!"

Red-Haired Xuân bowed low.

"I am deeply honored to serve you."

The woman smiled.

"What a refined gentleman!"

"Madame, what is family happiness if not the happiness of husbands and wives? What else can be done when love begins to fade?"

"You're right! If Mr. ILL continues to place restrictions on me, I may not be able to love him as when we were newly married."

"Madame, never mind what those old-fashioned moralists say; we do not only 'reform the outside.' Our society progresses according to the basic laws of evolution . . . During this deeply reformist era, everything conservative will be eliminated . . . Clothing should embellish one's natural beauty, not cover it up . . ."

Just as Red-Haired Xuân's speaking machine was shifting into high gear, the door to the shop swung open and the designer ran in, followed by the journalist. The designer raised his arms up over his head. "Oh! Our customs and morals have deteriorated so!"

He turned and gesticulated wildly at the journalist, who was busy thinking of how the designer was probably jealous because his wife was speaking to Red-Haired Xuân. (Artists are often jealous.) "You are right. It is truly unforgivable!"

"Don't you see what I mean? My wife? My own wife? My own wife dresses in the new modern way? My God! White pants? My God! Hair parted on the side and heart-shaped lipstick? Oh my god! What a slut! What a loose woman! What a—"

Red-Haired Xuân raised his hand to interrupt. "Sir, permit me to offer a defense of the gentler sex within the Europeanization Movement!"

The designer's wife started to grow angry. "Stop being so stupid! You call for renovation! You campaign for Europeanization! You demand that women reform themselves according to your wishes, to make themselves up following your methods! What about me? Yes, I am your wife, but I am also a woman! Everyone can see that I am a woman! Does anyone dare to say otherwise? Do any of you dare to say that I am not a woman?"

"We know, we know . . . Now shut up and stop misbehaving," said the designer.

He gestured for her to be quiet.

"I won't shut up! You can't make me!"

"Shut up, you idiot! Don't you know that there are different kinds of women? When we campaign for the reform of women, we mean other people's wives and sisters, not our own! Don't you understand? It's one thing for other women to reform, but you're my wife. Of course, I would never permit you to become one of those modern women!"

"But that's not fair," Mrs. ILL protested.

The designer turned to the journalist for help.

"Madame, we must make a distinction between our families and our society."

"Then why do you also advocate reform in your newspaper?"

"As your husband has explained already, when we speak about women, we mean the wives and sisters of other people, not our own wives and sisters. My family follows the old traditions. Our women cannot be allowed to wear modern clothes or to go dancing one day and to some festival the next. At home they must never be allowed to employ theories of liberation and equal rights to challenge the authority of their mothers-in-law."

The journalist's oh-so-progressive words inspired the designer.

"In my opinion, certain women ought to be confined to their rooms, get it?"

"Oh my god! You can't mean it!?" screamed the designer's wife.

"What is so difficult to understand?" replied the journalist, raising his two hands.

"What an ill-behaved woman!" added the designer bitterly. "Everything is so simple for your kind. You demand one fashion today and a different one the next! What a waste! You are nothing more than a parasite! After you squander all of your miserable husband's money on new clothes, what will you do when another outfit strikes your fancy? Prostitute yourself? Don't be such a copycat! Don't be such a slut!"

The designer thrust his finger into Xuân's face. "I caught you in the act! You were trying to corrupt my wife, to lead her astray with your silver tongue! You are trying to destroy my family! Watch out! I warn you . . ."

He grabbed his wife by the arm and dragged her to the door. "Hurry home!" he scowled. "Go home and take off those white pants, immediately! Go now, or I will divorce you!"

The journalist grabbed his briefcase and followed the couple out of the shop.

Alone in the shop, Red-Haired Xuân was overcome with confusion. He simply could not follow the logic of the reform-minded tailor. Just as he began to wonder if his altercation with the designer might cost him his new job, an elegantly dressed middle-aged clerk entered the shop. He addressed Xuân in a low whisper. "Sir! Sir, I have sprouted horns on my head."

Red-Haired Xuân rubbed his eyes to check if he might be dreaming.

The man spoke to him again. "Yes, it's true. I am a horned husband."

"Do you really have horns?" asked Xuân fearfully.

"Yes, it's true."

Red-Haired Xuân reached out to touch the man's head. "You must be joking. I don't feel any horns."

"Sir, I am speaking figuratively. What I mean is that my wife has slept with another man!"

"No kidding!"

"It's true. According to the French, husbands such as I are known as horned husbands. My wife is so immoral. I just want to kill myself!"

"Right now?"

"But I must do something glorious first, and for that I will need your help."

"But I don't even know who you are, Sir."

"I am a senior clerk at the post office. That is all you need to know. I am also a relative of Mr. Civilization. I was told by Mrs. Deputy Customs Officer that you are intelligent, educated, and generous. I have stopped by on my way to work to ask for your assistance."

"What can I do?"

"Very little, Sir, I promise. The next time you see me—and it will be soon, I assure you—point to my face and say: 'Sir, you have sprouted horns.' That is all."

"I don't know if I dare. Why must you draw attention to your horns in such an obvious way?"

"I beg of you. Help me, and I will pay you ten piasters! Here is an advance of five piasters."

The man slipped a five piaster note into Xuân's hand and moving furtively—as all horned husbands tend to do—he left the shop.

Chapter 6

Tennis Court Problems Again
●
Life in a Civilized Family
●
Red-Haired Xuân Leaps into Science

Three people stood at the window peering down into the yard.

"See what I mean!" exclaimed Mrs. Deputy Customs Officer. "Three workers and almost nothing has been done! God only knows when the tennis court will be finished!"

"Calm down, Auntie," said Mr. Civilization. "You can't build a tennis court overnight."

"There's no hurry," added Mrs. Civilization. "We can start practicing as soon as it's done."

The tennis court was being made from fragments of brick and several layers of *bích toong*.[1] The hard rectangular surface was surrounded by dug-up lemon trees, rose bushes, and piles of grass and weeds. In addition to her newfound passion for sports, there was another reason why Mrs. Deputy Customs Officer had ordered her flower garden dug up and replaced by a tennis court. But it was a reason known only to God.

"Almost eight hundred piasters for a tennis court. Is that a good price?"

"It seems reasonable to me, Auntie," Mrs. Civilization said reassuringly. "Most sports clubs hold dozens of fund-raisers before they can build a single court. Eight-hundred seems like a decent price."

---

1. *Béton* (concrete).

Because he assumed that Mrs. Deputy Customs Officer was building the court out of passion for sports, on the one hand, and love for her niece—his wife—on the other, Mr. Civilization felt compelled to reassure her as well. "So what if it's a little expensive. This court might change your life. Perhaps your house will become like a club—a meeting place where upper-class intellectuals gather together to improve and help civilize our society! It will not only enhance your reputation, Auntie, but it will improve the future prospects of little brother Blessing. Children today need a variety of civilizing influences. They need physical instruction as well as spiritual guidance. In the past our elders focused exclusively on the cultivation of the mind—a serious mistake in my opinion."

He spoke elegantly, fluently, and, for someone who didn't actually believe what he was saying, with great conviction. Although Mrs. Deputy Customs Officer failed to grasp his point, she was pleased because it sounded, at least, like they were of the same mind. But why in the world did he think that her tennis court would help civilize the society?

They returned to the living room.

"That Xuân seems pretty efficient, huh?" said Mrs. Deputy Customs Officer.

"He is very intelligent, indeed!" her niece replied. "He is already a big hit among our customers."

"He is blessed with good luck!" said Mrs. Deputy Customs Officer. "Joy and prosperity blossom wherever he goes."

"I think you are right! Since he started with us, our sales are way up."

"He is well spoken and quick on his feet, too," her nephew-in-law added.

"Some people are cursed with bad luck, but fortune follows him wherever he goes. It must be fate. Too bad he was orphaned as a child. With a bit of schooling, he could be an educated person."

"I couldn't disagree more," Mr. Civilization protested. "What does he have to complain about? Ball boys and tailor's assistants can also contribute to social progress! Moreover, if he ever makes a name for himself, being an orphan will only enhance his reputation! Who cares if the son of a rich mandarin gains fame and fortune? He ought to be proud to be a member of the common people; they are respected the world over! The aristocracy and the bourgeois are out nowadays, and the common people are in. Hooray for the common people! Long live the common people!"

The more he spoke, the more Mrs. Deputy Customs Officer found her nephew-in-law to be civilized, up-to-date, and more than deserving of the exalted title foreign exchange student, even though he had never earned the diploma. She yawned and hugged Lulu in a passionate embrace. "Where is everyone? They said they would come over today."

Mr. Civilization leaned back in his chair and looked up at the ceiling. He put the eighteenth *Ăng-lê*[2] cigarette of the day into his mouth and struck a match. Being a fashionable woman, his wife put both of her feet up on the low coffee table.

"Where is everyone this afternoon?" she repeated.

"Some of my friends may come over later today."

"Whom do you mean, my dear?"

"The new group or the older one?" asked Mrs. Deputy Customs Officer.

"Just a couple of friends—Dr. Straight Talk, Joseph Thiết, maybe several others."

"Really!"

"I think you've met them before, Auntie. They plan to make a courtesy call."

"Very good!" Mrs. Deputy Customs Officer replied.

She buzzed for the cook, who entered promptly.

"Go buy ice for drinks!" she ordered. "Open wide the main entrance! Chain the dogs. Hurry up!"

Gusts from the ceiling fan rustled the cigarette paper–thin clothes covering the white skin of the two fashionable ladies. The ticking of the clock drew attention to the silence in the room. Looking like the soul of Vietnam on the road of evolution and liberation, Mrs. Deputy Customs Officer hugged her French puppy and gazed up dreamily at the ceiling fan. Mr. and Mrs. Civilization, on the other hand, looked worn-out from the crushing burdens of pursuing life's four essential pleasures (eating, sleeping, making love, and going to the toilet) in a civilized way and promoting populism.

The doorbell rang out, jolting the hostess from her chair. Moments later, an old man entered the room. The Civilizations stood up, and

---

2. *Anglais* (English).

Mrs. Deputy Customs Officer offered a warm greeting. "Welcome! What a surprise and honor that you have stopped by to visit us, Grandpa Hồng."

Before he could reply, Grandpa Hồng was seized by a fit of violent coughing. It sounded as if he were choking on a water pipe. Although it was the middle of summer, he wore a padded coat and heavy leather shoes. He smelled of peppermint oil and wore several medals pinned to his chest.

Mr. Civilization looked uneasily at his wife, embarrassed at the fact that Grandpa Hồng was his father. In the past he had been a senior clerk—an exemplary official and loyal citizen of the protectorate. He was also a kind-hearted father who feared and slavishly indulged his spoiled children. Following retirement, the state acknowledged his thirty years of service to the king and the country by awarding him the Hồng Lô Tự Thiếu Khanh medal.[3] Like many Vietnamese of the era, he was also an opium addict.

Grandpa Hồng's only ambition in life was to become a great-grandpa. In pursuit of this worthy goal, he contrived to behave like an old man on his last legs, although in truth he was no more than fifty. Whenever he went out, he wore a heavy *ba đờ xuy*,[4] whether it was winter or not. To advertise his senility, he coughed uncontrollably during rickshaw rides and always made a point to miscalculate the fare. If anyone tried to speak with him while he was preparing his opium, he would close his eyes, frown, and say: "I know! I know! What a pain! Shut up, already!" He said this as a matter of principle, even as he listened attentively.

As with many rich people who squandered money for their children to "study" in France, Grandpa Hồng respected his son and offered up stories about him as if he were serving an elegant *đét-se*.[5] While disappointed that his son had returned home without a diploma, he was reassured by the argument that "education does not come from a diploma. If it did, then even Phạm Quỳnh and Nguyễn Văn Vĩnh are uneducated."[6] He was also thrilled that his son had become a revolutionary within the prevailing legal framework. This allowed Mr. Civilization to radically reform society without being

---

3. Medal of Work and Social Merit.
4. *Pardessus* (overcoat).
5. Dessert.
6. Phạm Quỳnh (1898–1945) and Nguyễn Văn Vĩnh (1882–1936) were prominent francophone intellectuals and journalists during the interwar era.

jailed or executed. He was especially proud that his son had not become one of those silly revolutionaries who aspires to bring happiness to the people without teaching them about dancing or ultramodern clothes. Like many old and stupid people, Grandpa Hồng did not allow his utter ignorance of civilization to prevent him from supporting its merits wholeheartedly. Just as he was faithful to Great France, Grandpa Hồng was fiercely loyal to his son, a fidelity he demonstrated by adopting all of his son's many foreign affectations, such as using the pronouns *toa* and *moa*.[7]

Mrs. Deputy Customs Officer offered her arm to Grandpa Hồng. With her assistance, he took his seat—but gingerly, like a genuine great-grandpa.

"When did *toa* arrive here?" he asked his son.

"A while ago," Mr. Civilization answered, as if not addressing anyone in particular.

"*Moa* has some business with *toa*. Our *via*[8] seems on the verge of . . . going . . . of leaving us. Perhaps we ought to find a medical doctor so that old *via* can enjoy a little French science before he dies . . ."

"Just how sick is Great-Grandpa?" Mrs. Deputy Customs Officer asked.

Grandpa Hồng coughed for several moments. "It's very serious! He's over eighty years old, you know."

"To live this long seems a violation of Heaven's will," Mrs. Civilization said angrily.

"I had hoped that the old man would have passed on already," Grandpa Hồng explained apologetically. "The sooner, the better. Why continue living when you can no longer eat or sleep and all you can do is whine and wet the bed? It will also be a sign of bad luck for our family if I die before the old man. If, on the other hand, he dies first, I will be able to stage a lavish and solemn funeral for a huge number of guests."

"Then, why call a doctor?" Mrs. Deputy Customs Officer asked, stifling a nervous giggle.

"We must call one. Better that the old man dies because of a doctor than because of a lack of medicine. Anyway, we will try to find one of those doctors who is more likely to kill him than cure him."

---

7. *Toi* and *Moi* (you and I).
8. *Vieux* (old man).

"In that case there is no point looking for an accomplished doctor," Mr. Civilization said in a loud and dignified voice.

"Indeed. Any quack will do just fine," Grandpa Hồng added. "Does *toa* know of any really second-rate doctors among your old friends?"

Mr. Civilization sat down and scratched his head pensively as if planning some sort of high-tech assassination. "*Moa* has a friend who opened a clinic two years ago. He returned home on the same ship with *moa*. I hear that many people have died under his care. One patient who came to him with a small pimple on his chin died after he treated it with Chinese herbs. His reputation for quackery is unrivaled."

"Isn't he the one who tried to deflower one of his female patients . . . ?" asked Mrs. Civilization.

"That's right," Mr. Civilization nodded.

"Who is he, again? What was his name?" Mrs. Deputy Customs Officer asked with sudden interest.

Grandpa Hồng ignored the question.

"We only need an unscrupulous doctor—someone who neglects his patients or perhaps . . . overmedicates them. That should be enough for the *via*."

"Great-Grandpa is well over eighty," put in Mrs. Deputy Customs Officer. "Maybe the answer is to call a pediatrician. Or we could get an optometrist for his stomach aches or a V.D. specialist for his asthma."

She paused for a moment. "I guess there's no point getting that deflowerer for a sick old man."

Grandpa Hồng frowned. "The problem, of course, is that it's not clear that the old man actually has any illness."

"Father," Mrs. Civilization began respectfully. "We must be very careful here. What if we get a cardiologist and the old man turns out to really have a heart problem?"

At that moment Red-Haired Xuân timidly entered the room. He was barely acknowledged and sat down beside a large mirror, where he could stare admiringly at his European-style suit. He had bought it with the five piasters given him by the senior postal clerk.

"Long live horned husbands!" he thought merrily to himself. "Horns for everybody!"

Mrs. Deputy Customs Officer turned to Grandpa Hồng. "Alright, so Great-Grandpa has no reported illnesses, but he must have some pains . . . or a little discomfort at least!"

"A lot!" responded Grandpa Hồng. "He coughs, spits, and whines all day and night! Sometimes he complains of stomach pains."

At that Red-Haired Xuân entered the conversation. "Does the patient ever have trouble breathing?" he asked. "Does he ever seem congested?"

"Sometimes, yes," Grandpa Hồng replied.

"It sounds like asthma. A little ambergris should clear that up."

"But what about his stomach pains?"

"The patient has two diseases," Xuân replied, sounding like a real herbalist. "He is doubtless very old. His stomach aches come from poor blood circulation that prevents him from digesting his food. It could also derive from too many vapors in the sperm following sexual intercourse. Of course, sometimes such pain is merely psychosomatic. There are also cases in which the pain migrates from the patient's stomach to his spine. Do you know if his pain is greater before he eats or afterwards?"

"Afterwards, I think."

"I see. In that case his intestines probably lack sour fluids. People short of sour fluids typically hurt when they are full. Those with an abundance of sour fluids tend to hurt when they are hungry."

Red-Haired Xuân rattled on like a well-oiled diagnostic machine. Mrs. Deputy Customs Officer and Mr. and Mrs. Civilization listened in stunned silence. How strange! How utterly unexpected!

"Sir, where did you develop such an extensive medical knowledge?" Grandpa Hồng asked respectfully.

Before he could respond, Mr. Civilization cut him off. "This is a friend of mine—a student from the medical school. I forgot to introduce him to you, father."

How unexpected, indeed!

How could Xuân have guessed the benefit he was to derive from an old part-time job for which he was paid to sit on the hood of a car, made up as Charlot,[9] and bark out advertisements over a loudspeaker for herbal medicine manufactured by the self-proclaimed Cochinchinese King of Venereal Disease Treatment. It was from this humble origin that Xuân set off on the road to science, status, and prosperity.

---

9. Charlie Chaplain.

Chapter 7

A Living Person's Will

❧

A Scientific Debate

❧

Love—What Else Are You Waiting For?

Reclining atop an ornate ebony bed encrusted with mother-of-pearl, Grandpa Hồng closed his eyes. To his right lay an opium tray; to his left, a rickshaw coolie. Grandma sat at his feet. The rickshaw coolie wiped off his hooves, readying himself for the heavy responsibilities of preparing and serving opium.

"I will invite the herbalist," Grandma said.

Grandpa Hồng frowned and snapped at his wife for the tenth time that evening. "I know! I know! What a pain! Shut up, already!"

Grandma ignored him. "We should also start making funeral arrangements . . ."

"I know! I know! What a pain! Shut up, already!"

"I think we should have a combination of traditional and modern rites. Let's have a mourning flag, a paper and bamboo house for the ritual offering, a Chinese bugle, a sedan coffin, and several dozen banners with parallel verse. We can also have a Western trumpet to please the children, but I insist that we include the older rites as well."

"I know! I know! What a pain! Shut up, already!"

Grandma held her tongue. After several moments Grandpa could not bear her silence any longer. "What else, Grandma?"

The rickshaw puller ignored this all-too-familiar exchange. Grandma continued to list all the complicated rites she wanted. And

Grandpa continued to retch. As usual, the complexity of the funeral arrangements and the anxiety over how they would be perceived overwhelmed any sentimental meaning invested in the event. Outside in the living room, far from the ornate ebony bed, a small group of guests gathered including friends and relatives of the Civilizations. Each of them had already ascended the stairs, entered the room where Great-Grandpa lay, lifted the mosquito net, and peeked inside. Then, with their duty complete, they rushed downstairs to drink tea, smoke, and exchange bits of gossip—all the time contemplating the percentage of the old man's fortune they were due upon his death. Although the old man was only moderately sick, he was now referred to in the past tense.

By this time Mr. ILL was busy designing several ultramodern mourning outfits. The journalist was preparing an obituary, a funeral notice, and photos for the newspaper. Mrs. Civilization was imagining how she might look in all-white mourning clothes, a fashion opportunity that she had been dreaming of for some time. Mr. Civilization sat, smoking his Ăng-lê cigarettes, thinking of the property he was to inherit when the old man finally bit the dust. With the help of his lawyer, the old man had prepared a will, which stipulated that the profit derived from the several dozen houses that he owned would be split among his children and grandchildren, but only after he died. He was blissfully unaware that this will had only enhanced a powerful desire among his children and grandchildren for his demise. In the past he had made his fortune with his bare hands. He had worked his entire life for his family, and now death had become his final filial obligation.

Young Mr. Tân tinkered busily with several cameras, trying to decide which one to use during the funeral. Everyone called him Tân the High School Graduate, not because he had graduated from high school but because he had failed the graduation exam on three separate occasions. Mrs. Deputy Customs Officer was holding her sacred son like a gentle mother. Mr. Joseph Thiết, a close friend of Mr. Civilization, was contemplating starting up a royalist newspaper, not for the imperial court in Huế but for Mr. Léon Daudet and the Orléans family in France. He viewed the upcoming funeral as an opportunity to boast about his past exploits.

"I remember when Monsieur Banville passed away," he began. "It seemed that half of Paris turned out for his funeral, including all the

right-wing parties. Back then, I was a member of the Thập tự
Lửa[1] . . ."

But no one listened to him. They were much too busy listening to
Mr. ILL.

"The funeral clothes must be made from white Shanghai crepe
with a black border. The collar will be rose shaped—white petals
with black trim! The same goes for the mourning cap! White with
black trim looks better than black with white trim."

"It's going to look gorgeous!" exclaimed Mrs. Deputy Customs
Officer. "It makes you look forward to funerals!"

Little Master Blessing was less impressed. "No way!"

Mrs. Civilization clapped her elegant hands together.

"Very good! *Dernière création!*"[2]

Only the horned senior clerk was silent. There was still no sign of
his wife. His eyes welled up with hatred. He looked around for
Xuân but could not find him either.

"Where is Mr. Xuân?" he asked Mr. Civilization.

"He's getting some medicine. He should be back soon."

The discussion turned to the question of which profession and
position ought to be printed in the obituary. As the debate heated
up, Miss Snow—Grandpa Hồng's eighteen-year-old baby daughter—entered the room. She was beautiful and possessed a frivolous
romantic quality that was fashionable for the time.

"I've come from the homes of two different herbalists," she announced, "but I didn't meet either of them. I left messages for them
to come over as soon as they can."

"Damn it!" screamed Grandma from somewhere in the room.
"You silly child! They will never forgive our family if you invite two
at the same time!"

"Why, for Heaven's sake, did you invite two herbalists?" Mr.
Civilization added angrily. "I said that we should wait for Mr. Xuân
to bring back the sacred medicine from the Bia Pagoda . . ."

"My God!" interjected Joseph Thiết. "If *toa* relies on medicine
from the Bia Pagoda, then *toa* is truly crazy!"

"*Toi* doesn't understand! Nothing is more important than the pa-

---

1. Croix de Feu—a right-wing party in interwar France founded initially as a veter-
ans' organization in 1920.
2. Most recent creation.

tient's belief in the medicine. Haven't *toi* heard about the healing powers of positive thinking? Only faith can cure. And *moi*'s old man has great faith in the sacred medicine of the Bia Pagoda . . ."

"But I thought the old man was being treated by Mr. Xuân, a student from the medical college!"

"Indeed, he is," explained Mr. Civilization. "The old man has spoken with Mr. Xuân and appears to respect him deeply. He has great faith in him. It seems that Mr. Xuân also believes in the healing powers of the sacred medicine from the Bia Pagoda. How can *moa* old man not recover? Such concentrated faith is enough to empower any quack."

"It makes sense to me," said Joseph Thiết, not aware of his friend's ulterior motives.

Mr. Civilization continued to attack his younger sister. "Who gave you permission to invite those two herbalists, little girl?"

"It was Mother," she protested. "I only did what Mother told me to do."

Mr. Civilization ran into the other room, looking for his mother.

"Oh, no!" he moaned under his breath. "What a pain! A little medicine is usually all you need to do a patient in. But too many cooks may spoil the soup! Don't you know that saying, Mother?"

Grandma, who was still worried about the arrival of the two rival herbalists, offered a suggestion. "Perhaps we should let each doctor prescribe something."

"I know! I know! What a pain! Shut up, already!" Grandpa snapped.

"Otherwise," Grandma continued, "they will be angry and refuse to come over when someone is really sick."

Amid all this chaos Red-Haired Xuân entered with a vial of filthy water tucked under his arm and a bundle of strange leaves in his hand. His eyes fell on the senior clerk, which triggered thoughts of his new European suit, which in turn prompted him to appreciate the importance of always trying to meet one's obligations. He cleared his throat to draw attention to himself.

"Sir," he said, pointing at the senior clerk, "you seem to h—."

But before he could finish the horned clerk gestured for him to hold off.

The guests greeted Xuân like a returning prince. They gathered around him and asked about his trip to the Bia Pagoda. Miss Snow and her innocent-looking eyes were especially attentive to Xuân, having heard from her brother that he was a student from the medical college.

"Ladies and gentlemen," said Mr. Civilization with both his eyes and Adam's apple bulging, "you are all invited upstairs to witness the administration of the sacred medicine."

As the assembled crowd headed toward the stairs, two elderly herbalists—Dr. Spleen and Dr. Lung—entered the front door almost simultaneously. They were followed by two rickshaw drivers, desperately trying to collect their fares. Miss Snow emerged from the crowd and gave them each several bills. Grandpa Hồng began shepherding the rest of the crowd upstairs.

At that moment there were only two people tending to Great-Grandpa: Mr. Two and his daughter Miss Moon. Although Mr. Two was Grandpa Hồng's younger brother, he lived in the countryside and, as a result, garnered little respect within the family. To him it seemed that his elder brother, his nephew, and his niece by marriage were aliens from another world. He never expressed this thought publicly, however, because he feared that it would reveal him to be an old-fashioned country bumpkin. Whenever Miss Moon returned home from her periodic trips to the city, Mr. Two dared not criticize the affectations of speech and behavior that she had picked up from the progressive, civilizing movement then raging throughout the country. Upon receiving the news that Great-Grandpa was ill, he rushed to his bedside in the city, where he remained day and night. He helped his father sit up and lie down, emptied his spittoon, and spoon-fed him porridge. He did not begrudge his older brother, Grandpa Hồng, for lying in bed and smoking opium all day or his nephews and nieces for ignoring the old man. In his mind their neglect of his father, simply afforded enhanced opportunities for him to fulfill his own filial duty.

The crowd shuffled upstairs into the room and assembled quietly around the bed. Mr. Civilization made room for Dr. Spleen and Dr. Lung beside the patient and brought over the pile of leaves and the vial of dirty water.

"Behold the sacred medicine from the Bia Pagoda. Dear doctors, while the progressive nature of human science is beyond doubt, its ability to save lives does not yet compare to the miraculous power of the saints."

Dr. Spleen examined the leaves. "Daisies and purslane!? Is that all?"

Dr. Lung held the vial of water up to the light. "What the hell is this? Pond water?"

Mr. Civilization looked over at Red-Haired Xuân. "That's all it is," Xuân responded immediately. "But, in this case, it's a powerful sacred medicine. I have consulted the yin-yang coins; they have suggested this treatment. I have seen thousands of people cured in this way."

"These curatives are redundant," Dr. Spleen said bitterly. "I prescribed and administered three doses already. The patient's recovery is well under way . . ."

"Dear colleague," Dr. Lung interjected, "I do not wish to question your success in this matter, but, if the patient had recovered fully, there would have been no need for the family to purchase curatives from the Bia Pagoda!"

Dr. Spleen snatched the vial of dirty water from the hands of Dr. Lung. "Let me see that!" he snapped. "This is not pond water! It's simply water from a rice field! If he drinks this water, he will be beyond recovery! There will be no patient left to cure."

"Are you talking to me?" protested Dr. Lung. "How dare you? It wasn't I who made that ridiculous prescription!"

But Dr. Spleen ignored his mistake. "So what if it's not your prescription? You identified it as pond water when it is clearly field water. Any true herbalist should be able to tell the difference!"

"Fine, I give up!" Dr. Lung pouted. "I guess that makes you the only qualified herbalist in the country!"

"My qualifications are none of your business!"

The famous herbalists stood face-to-face, their tempers simmering to a boil.

"I don't see why you are so damned arrogant! The funeral of Provincial Governor Vi was only two days ago!"

"Oh! Please! Provincial Governor Vi was over sixty when he died! You can't hold me responsible for what happened to him! But what about the case of that little girl . . . Chắt . . . the daughter of Mr. Vinh? She died after taking two of the doses that you prescribed!"

Dr. Lung stretched out his open palms defensively. "Who told you that? Who said she had taken only two doses? Was it my fault that she ate those plums when she had a fever? She would have been fine, otherwise! Two doses? Who was the bastard that pre-scribed that shoddy, two-bit stomach medicine for Đại the clerk? He almost died because of that! What kind of herbalist would do that? They should throw you in jail for that one! You charlatan!"

But Dr. Spleen did not flinch. "Charlatan? At least I haven't caused any miscarriages."

Dr. Lung's eyes bulged out like two stuffed snails. "How dare you!? Go ahead! Say something else! I dare you!"

"I'm not afraid of you! I'll say whatever I want! I'll say it to the French Security Police if I please! How would you like that!?"

"Don't you threaten me! I'll tell them about the time that you mas-saged the eyeball of one of your patients so much that it popped right out! You're the bastard responsible for that one! You're the bastard!"

"Can I help it if he was going blind? How about the time you tried to fix that little boy's asthma with that bogus ear-wood fungus? You kept at it for weeks with no results!"

"What about when Mrs. Deputy Customs Officer started her menopause and you thought she was pregnant?"

Mrs. Deputy Customs Officer stopped giggling and ran shame-faced out of the room. "You are truly cruel! How about when Miss Moon here had that problem with smelly armpits? You prescribed peppermint oil for over six months, and it still didn't work."

"Six months? You've been treating Miss Snow's mangy itch for over three years now!"

Miss Moon and Miss Snow stiffened abruptly, stopped their titter-ing, and, red-faced, exited the room together.

Mr. Civilization grabbed Dr. Spleen and dragged him down the stairs. Mr. Two hustled Dr. Lung out into the hall. Grandpa Hồng began his usual whining. "I know! I know! What a pain! Shut up, already!"

The others were either laughing hysterically or commiserating with Grandma about the doctor's public announcement of her daughter's mangy itch. The fight between the famous herbalists roused the eighty-year-old Great-Grandpa from his sleep. He awoke feeling fit and healthy.

"What's all this commotion?" he asked. "Am I awake, or is this some sort of dream?"

After expelling the famous herbalists from the house, Mr. Civiliza-tion returned and sat down beside the bed.

"Your children and grandchildren are happy because you have recovered, Great-Grandpa."

"I'm recovered? I'm not dead? I kowtow before Heaven!"

"You are all better now, Great-Grandpa, thanks to Dr. Xuân."

"What? Where is that medicine from the Bia Pagoda?"

"You've taken half of it already, Great-Grandpa. That's why you regained consciousness."

"Really?"

"Really, Great-Grandpa!"

Mr. Civilization winked at Xuân.

"Great-Grandpa," Xuân began, "I consulted the yin-yang coins . . . They foretold that Heaven would help the doctor that consulted its powers. Heaven ignores herbalists."

"Where is the rest of the medicine?" the old man asked eagerly.

Red-Haired Xuân handed over the field water and several daisy leaves.

"They say that the sacred medicine must come from a pond. It will only work if it is extremely dirty and stinky. Don't try to trick me. I am just an old man."

The old man swallowed a few leaves and downed several cap-fulls of field water. Sacred medicine, indeed! A half-hour later the old man had begun to regain his strength. He sat up and ate half a bowl of porridge.

After everyone had gone home or fallen asleep, Red-Haired Xuân and Miss Snow remained in the patient's room. Even Mr. Two was asleep on the sofa, content in the knowledge that the old man was on the road to recovery. For Miss Snow fulfilling her duty toward Great-Grandpa was little more than an excuse to stay up alone with Red-Haired Xuân. The two did not speak but exchanged a series of knowing glances. The patient slept quietly. He did not cough, spit up, or moan.

The moon shone brightly through the glass window.

Finally, Miss Snow boldly broke the silence. "Excuse me, Sir. That herbalist doctor lied. I . . . I . . . I got over that mangy itch long ago."

Red-Haired Xuân was too embarrassed to respond, and another awkward silence ensued.

"Medical students are so stuck up," Miss Snow thought to her-self, and, overcome with bitterness, she returned to her room.

Chapter 8

Victory for the Common People in the Europeanization Shop

❧

A Financial Plot

❧

A Love Plot

In only two weeks the Popular Movement had achieved a stunning victory.

Two weeks before, fate had inserted Red-Haired Xuân into the bourgeois family of Mr. Civilization. With each passing day, his prestige and influence grew. Almost effortlessly and without being truly aware of it, he was gradually becoming an important player in society. His stupidity was mistaken for a combination of courtesy and modesty, and it made him wildly popular. Now it was merely a waiting game; a simple matter of time before he was catapulted to the top.

Whenever the fortune-teller came over to praise Mrs. Deputy Customs Officer's fidelity to her late husbands and confirm that her son (No way!) was indeed a gift sent directly from Heaven, he always made a point to predict a prosperous and exalted future for Red-Haired Xuân. In turn, Mrs. Deputy Customs Officer boasted of Xuân's education and refinement to the horned senior clerk. The horned senior clerk pointed out repeatedly Xuân's youthful promise to Grandpa Hồng (I know! What a pain! Shut up, already). Grandpa Hồng reiterated approvingly to Grandma and Great-Grandpa that Xuân was a student from the medical college. And, of course, everyone repeated eagerly what they had heard from everyone else. To reap all of these unexpected accolades, Red-Haired Xuân had to do little more than occasionally praise the prowess of the fortune-teller.

The truth, it seems, was known only to the Civilizations, but they dared not disclose it for fear that it might reflect badly on them. How could they admit that Xuân was originally from a lower-class family, that he had worked as a ball boy at the tennis courts, and that he was fired from this lowly post for lewd and immoral behavior? What would such a revelation mean for the Europeanization Tailor Shop? What about Red-Haired Xuân's popularity among female customers who had come to admire his silver tongue, quick wit, and good humor? Such thoughts consumed Mrs. Civilization. Her husband, on the other hand, was preoccupied by the fact that he had lied to his status-conscious father about Red-Haired Xuân's credentials as a student from the medical college. Hence, although he resented Xuân for saving his grandfather with the sacred medicine from the Bia Pagoda—an unforgivable sin—he held his tongue about Xuân's real background. As for Grandpa Hồng (I know! What a pain!), despite his surprise and disappointment that the leaves and dirty water had actually cured his father, he dared not reveal his true bitterness toward Xuân. After all, his son kept reminding him that Xuân was a student from the medical college and his son-in-law—the horned senior clerk—lauded Xuân as someone who deserved respect for his high education and youthful promise.

Hence, Xuân's fortunes continued to rise. When addressed as "Doctor" by Grandma, Mr. Two, Miss Moon, Miss Snow, or Joseph Thiết, he simply smiled and kept silent. When Mrs. Deputy Customs Officer leered at him lustfully, he remained stoic and indifferent. Following Great-Grandpa's complete recovery, Grandma invited Xuân to a formal banquet in his honor. This ushered in a new era of freedom and equality in which Xuân became a habitual guest at parties held by Mrs. Deputy Customs Officer and the Civilizations.

Soon it was considered an honor to have Xuân as a dinner guest. Many people admired and respected him. Others envied and hated him, but this mattered little. There were also those, more significantly, who loved and desired him. After prolonged exposure to this bizarre atmosphere of respect, fear, and flattery, Red-Haired Xuân began to put on airs. As is often the case in a society in which modesty is disdained, the more snobbish Xuân became, the more respect he enjoyed. Even his silence was interpreted, by the tailors and seamstresses, as a sign of authority. Miss Snow worshiped him because Grandma worshiped him. It was rumored, in fact, that Grandpa Hồng (I know! What a pain!) was arranging secretly for Me Sừ¹ Xuân to marry his precious daughter, Miss Snow. Hence, he was flattered and doted upon by Mr. ILL, Joseph Thiết, Dr. Straight Talk, even High School Graduate Tân (Mr. Civilization's younger brother). Because everyone was either being fooled or trying to fool each other, they were all compelled to fear and respect Xuân.

What a great victory for the common people!

At two that afternoon Mrs. Deputy Customs Officer arrived by car at the tailor shop. She hoped to induce Xuân to accompany her to La journée des cavalières Hanoiennes,² a festival at West Lake. It was to be a grand affair, presided over by important figures in the political arena. Mrs. Deputy Customs Officer was surprised to find Xuân minding the shop by himself.

"Mr. Xuân?" she said respectfully. "Why not close the shop this afternoon?"

"Why should I close the shop?" Xuân replied breezily. "I can take care of things here on my own."

Mrs. Deputy Customs Officer was silent for a moment.

"Have you heard the big news, Mr. Xuân?"

"News?" he replied curtly.

"Oh, Mr. Xuân! Mr. Xuân! My tennis court is almost done."

"Good for you," he replied tersely.

Mrs. Deputy Customs Officer was surprised at the unusually abrupt way he spoke to her. She imagined that there must be a reason for his curtness that she had not yet fully grasped. Why else would he adopt such an insolent tone with her? Feeling somewhat awkward, she inquired again about the day's plans.

"Aren't you coming along to the festival today?"

"The Europeanization Movement can ill afford my absence, even for a single day."

"Where are all the seamstresses and tailors?"

"The seamstresses have left for the festival dressed in the mourn-

---

1. Monsieur.
2. Hanoi Dance Festival.

90

ing outfits that Mr. ILL designed for Great-Grandpa's funeral. The clothes were never worn, you may recall, because I saved Great-Grandpa's life . . . The seamstresses will exhibit the clothes like a squad of living mannequins. We need to *lăng-xê*[3] this new clothing line, after all. The tailors will be handing out leaflets for our shop at the festival."

"I planned to go together with the Civilizations; we would be pleased if you would join us."

"It seems, Madame, that they have left without you."

Red-Haired Xuân continued to respond in a casual and haughty tone. As he spoke, he fondled a large pair of rubber falsies that had been sent from France as a contribution to the Europeanization Movement of the Great Kingdom of Việt. This beautification instrument had arrived several days before in a pretty box, covered by a half-dozen layers of shiny wrapping paper. Mrs. Deputy Customs Officer looked on lustily as Xuân handled the dirty item. She noticed now that they were all alone in the big tailor shop, a rare opportunity indeed. Before she could bring the conversation around to the rubber breasts, however, little Master Blessing, who was waiting out in the car, burst into a hysterical cacophony of "No ways!" Heartbroken, she shook hands with Xuân and left the shop.

Xuân smiled to himself. He knew that Mrs. Deputy Customs Officer, although old, was even naughtier than an innocent young girl. A quick nod from him is all it would take! But she was so old . . . what would be the point? Unless, of course, there was some money in it! He recalled that the talented fortune-teller had predicted that he would be lucky in love this year. He thought of the money to be made if only he were to propose some sort of monetary arrangement with Mrs. Deputy Customs Officer. But he decided to bide his time. Inadvertently, Xuân had just discovered a principle that most philosophers only recognize after their hair turns white: the value of playing hard to get.

Xuân's cheerful reflections were interrupted by the arrival of the horned senior clerk. He staggered forlornly into the shop and extended his hand to Xuân in silence.

"You, Sir, are a horned husband!" Xuân announced, shaking his hand vigorously.

---

3. *Lancer* (to launch).

"Very good! Thank you . . . thank you a thousand times."

The horned senior clerk's gratitude appeared extremely heartfelt, as if this were the first time someone had dared to inform him of the devastating news of his wife's affair. But, in fact, he felt nothing. Moments later, however, he pulled up a chair and began to complain. "That loud and dignified voice is good. But next time I want you to say it when you see me together with my wife. It will be even better if Grandpa and Great-Grandpa are there as well . . ."

"How can I say such a thing in front of your wife, not to mention Grandpa Hồng or Great-Grandpa?"

"Why do you think I paid you that ten piasters?"

"In that case, perhaps I ought to return the money," Xuân said anxiously.

The senior clerk sprang to his feet.

"God, no! I will die first! I will kill myself," he screamed.

"Please, no!" Xuân replied desperately. "But why do you need me to . . . expose your horns?"

But the senior clerk was too worked up to explain. "No! Don't do this to me! You promised! It's not right to break a promise. Plus, you must know that your position in the family is far from stable."

"Far from stable?" repeated Xuân in a worried voice.

"But, of course! You must be aware of the myriad reasons why Mr. ILL is jealous of you. One is that he blames you for spoiling his wife. Another is that you are better at waiting on customers than he is. Your skill at taking measurements for custom-made clothes is clearly superior. He fears that you are usurping his power. Mrs. Deputy Customs Officer seems annoyed with you as well, although I haven't yet figured out why. Not only do the Civilizations despise you secretly, but they seem to consider you a mortal enemy. And do you know why? It is because you saved Great-Grandpa's life, on the one hand, and made Miss Snow cancel an arranged marriage, on the other. I would be careful if I were you! As a close friend, it is my duty to warn you of these matters . . . In return, you must honor your obligation to me. Agreed?"

"But what should I do?"

"You must do what I say. It will, in fact, kill two birds with one stone."

"What do you mean?"

"Do what I say, and you will not only honor your obligation to me, but you will regain the love of those who now hate you."

"Hate me? How can they hate me for saving Great-Grandpa's life?"

"Only Grandma appreciated that. But she is powerless. More important are Grandpa Hồng and Mr. and Mrs. Civilization."

"But must I call attention to your horns in front of both your wife and Great-Grandpa?"

"Yes, indeed! The shock of the news will surely kill Great-Grandpa immediately . . . Then everyone will be rich, including me . . ."

"Is that true?"

"You will see. And don't worry—you will get your share as well."

Xuân hesitated for a moment. Then he shook his head. "I just can't! It's murder! I'm not a murderer! A criminal! No, I can't do it!"

"Think of it this way. If you help to kill this one person, it will make many persons extremely happy. That makes it worthwhile. Also, if you don't do it, then, sooner or later, you will be sacked."

Red-Haired Xuân extended his hand to the horned senior clerk. "I give you my promise, again . . . on my honor . . ."

The senior clerk grasped Xuân's hand tightly and eagerly. "I must go to work. Thank you in advance!"

As soon as he left, the door swung open again, and a beautiful woman rushed in. At first Xuân thought that it might be a fashionable young lady looking to get something tailor-made, but it turned out to be only Miss Snow.

"Did the senior clerk see me?" she asked breathlessly.

"I don't think so." Xuân responded.

"Thank goodness! Has everyone gone out?"

"They have. Aren't you going to join them at West Lake?"

"I don't want to go! There will be many singing girls and dancing girls there. They dress as fashionably as I, sometimes even more so. I'm from a respectable family. What if people mistake me for a dancing girl?"

"Quite right."

"Of course, that doesn't mean that I don't know how to dance. I do! I really do!"

"Yes, of course you do . . ."

"Can you dance, Mr. Xuân? C'mon, let's tango!"

Xuân was frightened.

"Another time perhaps . . . There is no music here. Wouldn't you prefer to go to a dancing hall . . . one day?"

"A dancing hall? Really? You promise? Imagine me, dancing with a snobbish medical student!?"

"You misunderstand me, Miss! Please don't think of me as snobbish. Just because I don't say very much, it doesn't mean that I am being disrespectful. How could I not respect you, Miss? I thank heaven that you don't despise me."

Xuân's subtle come-on, his first attempt ever with Miss Snow, impressed her deeply.

To conceal her emotions, she pointed inquisitively toward the pile of rubber breasts. "What are those, Mr. Xuân?"

"They are rubber breasts . . . they are for women who are progressive, civilized, and Europeanized."

"Really! I must tell my girlfriends. I have many modern ones, you know. I'm sure they will all flock to the Europeanization Tailor Shop."

"I don't believe you have any need for them," Xuân responded suggestively.

Miss Snow thrust her chest forward. "You think so? Do you think they are pert enough? They are rather unusual for a modern girl. And they are real, not rubber!"

As further confirmation that she was, in fact, civilized and modern, Miss Snow stepped boldly toward Xuân. "I give you permission to examine them!"

Red-Haired Xuân put his hands mischievously behind his back. "How can one tell what is real these days? Everything is so artificial! Love is artificial! Modernity is artificial! Even conservatism is artificial!"

"Then go ahead," said Miss Snow angrily. "Examine mine and see . . . see for yourself if they are artificial!"

Xuân looked around the empty store and peered out the window. Then he cupped Miss Snow's breasts in his hands, trying to determine their authenticity. When he was satisfied that they were, in fact, the genuine article, he kissed her gently on the hand. "They are indeed authentic—a true rarity in this artificial life."

Miss Snow was very moved and sighed deeply. "I wonder if you might help me with something," she said softly. "I'd be ever so grateful."

"It would be an honor!"

"I do not want to marry my fiancé. I know that he will sprout horns if I am forced to marry him. He is nothing like you! He is from the countryside, and I fear that he will not know how to love me in a civilized way. It's a real shame."

"What can I do?"

"Perhaps . . . perhaps you can pretend that you are courting me . . . If we pretend that we are romantically involved, my fiancé will be forced to leave me. Understand? We will only pretend! For this plan to work, I need to be dishonored, to be thought of as a bad girl."

"Is that so?"

"Of course, you will be dishonored as well, as the defiler of my virginity!"

"If you promise not to give me horns in the future, I would be willing to do more than just pretend to dishonor you. I would be willing to actually defile your virginity."

"Doctor! Do you mean it?"

"It would be my great honor to be the cause of your dishonor."

"Oh, thank you! I love you so much! But you must ask for some time off. How many days will you need to dishonor a respectable and well-behaved girl like myself?"

For the rest of the afternoon they continued the discussion— Xuân, man of the common people, and Miss Snow, the modern woman.

Chapter 9

A Real-Life Fairyland
➰
The Philosophy of an Adulteress
➰
An Example of "Semi-Virginity"

To the west of Hanoi lies a lake, recently divided into two smaller lakes separated by a single road known as Old Fish Road. The road is famous throughout the country—all twenty million of our compatriots know of it—because it is here that girls from good and not-so-good families go out with young male college students, law students, and students without institutional affiliation. They come to this road night after night to flirt with each other and to transgress the rules of each other's families. After several months they invariably jump together into one of the lakes.

Initially, most people jumped into West Lake, but, because it was very deep, few of those who attempted suicide survived. Hence, people eventually shifted to the more shallow and less dangerous White Bamboo Lake. Another reason for the growth in popularity of the White Bamboo Lake was the state's clever decision to post billboards that read, "No Garbage in West Lake."

Night after night idle rickshaw pullers and jobless young men who could swim loitered around the banks of the lake. There they waited expectantly for a heart-rending and plaintive "Save me!" whereupon they would dive into the waters and fish out a beautiful girl. Next stop was the Hàng Đậu Police Station, where they would receive a monetary award, pose for newspaper photos, and sit through numerous noisy interviews. As a result, White Bamboo Lake became an important setting for those awful tragedies staged regularly in Hanoi during which the evil Vietnamese family conspires to prevent free marriage, free divorce, free remarriage, and so on.

The White Bamboo Lake might have remained forever and ever little more than a contemporary barometer of tragic conflict between the Old and the New, the Individual and the Family, Self-Sacrifice and Political Awakening, and Oppression and Liberation, had not a great patriot decided to construct on its banks an irresistible (even to the French) lakeside inn known as the Fairyland Hotel. On the day the hotel opened, the Protectorate attempted to purify and exorcize the atmosphere surrounding the lake by ordering schoolgirls to practice a special dance in which they performed as fairies who descend to earth and release the souls of those who had actually died during their suicide attempts. As a result, the Fairyland Hotel became as well known as Old Fish Road and White Bamboo Lake. All self-respecting Vietnamese felt obliged to stay at the hotel at least once, in order to avoid being chided by fashionable intellectuals for forsaking their roots or losing their country to foreigners.

Given the liberationist ideology of Miss Snow, it is no surprise that she saw the hotel as the perfect site to be dishonored. For Xuân it was as good a place as any to fulfill his solemn obligation of defiling the virginity of a respectable girl. They entered the hotel through the Japanese-style concrete gate.

"We will rent a room together, my dear!" Miss Snow said to Xuân. "We will eat together, drink together, and dance together! We will play Ping-Pong and go boating together. Everyone must see us together."

Xuân racked his brain for a flowery reply, but he could only come up with a sentence that Mr. ILL used frequently with female customers in the tailor shop.

"We are honored to serve you, Madame."

Xuân's flat delivery and straight face made Miss Snow think he was making a joke. She burst out laughing in a way common among fashionable women. "Oh, my goodness! What a sense of humor you have, Doctor!"

They sauntered leisurely through the hotel flower garden, as natural as any pair of secret lovers.

"Before we rent a room, let's take a tour of Fairyland!" Miss Snow whispered to Xuân.

The Fairyland Hotel was, indeed, a magnificent castle. For Vietnamese who had money to burn it possessed anything and everything that might possibly bring happiness. A team of architects had employed all of their creative energy to erect an extraordinary building overhanging the lake. Its numerous balconies were constructed so that guests might be able to watch each other boating and swimming. Its huge garden contained a tennis court, Ping-Pong tables, and a swimming pool. There was a dancehall and a wireless radio room. The restaurant specialized in French and Chinese cuisine and served all manner of rare and expensive delicacies. For those who could afford the bill, a night in the hotel offered all the pleasures of modern life presented in an atmosphere as refined as the old imperial capital. If the Fairyland Hotel did not exist, how could the Vietnamese hold up their heads among foreigners? The hotel provided a perfect place for the idle bourgeois to come together and forget their ennui. It contained sixty rooms and dozens of young female love peddlers (also known as top-grade quality hens), following a system innovated in more civilized countries.

When Xuân and Miss Snow arrived at eight o'clock Sunday morning, the hotel was relatively empty. There were a few people on the tennis courts and several others playing Ping-Pong. Half a dozen elegantly dressed men and women sat drinking on a balcony looking out over the lake. Three glamorous hotel hens, dressed as upperclass girls, lolled about looking for men with whom to go swimming. Everyone was chatting merrily.

A modern-looking girl extended her hand to Xuân and Miss Snow and started introducing them to the other guests. "Allow me to introduce Mr. Xuân, the manager of the Europeanization Tailor Shop, a skillful measurer of women, and a designer who has created many beautiful and fashionable outfits. We women have benefited greatly from his talents."

"You must be a colleague of Mr. ILL," a young man said, respectfully.

"That is correct."

At that moment the hotel owner appeared, all dressed up as if for a big party. Red-Haired Xuân blanched and looked around for a place to hide. Miss Snow stepped forward to introduce them.

"Doctor Xuân, my boyfriend . . . Mr. Victor Ban, the owner of Fairyland . . ."

Victor Ban bowed his head low and shook hands with Xuân, who stood frozen in place like a wooden statue. Just like Xuân, Victor Ban had also recently reinvented himself—from the King of Venereal Disease Treatment to the owner of the Fairyland Hotel. But Xuân's transformation—he was now a doctor—was quite unbelievable!

After a stint as an unsuccessful horse jockey, Mr. Victor Ban realized that the tides of civilization sweeping over our country were to be accompanied by waves of venereal disease. He decided to change his job. Mixing cat jelly with eucalyptus oil and little bits of clay, he fashioned a relatively effective treatment for the affliction. As with other self-respecting Kings of Venereal Disease Treatment, his cures rarely lasted as long as advertised. But, nevertheless, within two years he had become a millionaire. Flush with capital, he quickly built a large brothel outside of the city center and hired ten prostitutes. Every time a young, healthy man began frequenting his brothel, they would eventually be directed by one of the working girls to the clinic of Victor Ban. Temporarily cured, they would visit the brothel again, creating a sort of continuous shuttle service between the brothel and the clinic. Victor Ban grew richer and richer. His agents worked in all three regions of the country. His cars canvassed every street, broadcasting incessantly over loudspeakers on the unchecked spread of nocturnal emissions, wet dreams, chilly semen, painful vaginal discharge, syphilis, and gonorrhea. In addition, he treated perforated lungs, ripped intestines, heart illnesses, eye problems, and various ear ailments. His jingles were so pervasive and persuasive that healthy people feared for their lives, purchased his medicines, and sung his praises as a patriot and a great humanitarian. Among our twenty million compatriots, Victor Ban had become a household name . . . Soon thereafter, he plotted to create a place of refuge—a fairyland—within this venereal disease–infested land so that the people might forget their painful and stinking sores. Hence, he opened the Fairyland Hotel.

It was only a few years ago that he had paid a bastard and vagabond—now Dr. Xuân—twenty cents per day to sit on the hood of his cars and scream into the loudspeaker: "Wet dreams, syphilis . . ." It was almost beyond belief! This same Xuân was now the boyfriend of Grandpa Hồng's youngest daughter, Miss Snow, and a respected doctor.

Xuân and Victor Ban stood staring at each other. Luckily for Xuân, they were interrupted by one of the modern girls. "How is business at the tailor shop?"

"It is the busiest store around!" Miss Snow replied. "It is so good that Xuân has quit medical school. They teach nothing of value there anyway! It's a waste of time. Now he has more time for *ten-nít.*"[1]

During the conversation a young man had been staring at Xuân's red hair. "Which kind of dye you use in your hair, Sir? It's beautiful. Very fashionable! I want to dye my hair too, but I haven't found a good brand . . . I'd like a perm as well."

"Come to my shop, and I will suggest a product that should work for you," Xuân replied.

"Now, now!" said the girl, chiding the man and flattering Miss Snow simultaneously. "Mr. Xuân's job is to promote the latest fashions and most elegant styles. Beautiful hair is just part of the whole package. Everyone knows that!"

Mr. Victor Ban turned to Miss Snow. "Do you plan to stay here all day or only for a brief stay?"

She elbowed Xuân in the side. "What do you think, boyfriend? Just one day? Maybe it will be more fun to stay longer?"

Xuân tried to calculate how long it might take to defile the honor of a respectable girl. "Let's decide after lunch."

Victor Ban excused himself. Another elegantly dressed young man approached the group and addressed Xuân.

"I would be honored if you would play a *séc*[2] with me," he said.

Xuân agreed, and everybody moved to the tennis court. It took less than an hour for Red-Haired Xuân to defeat the young man. The crowd applauded, and Miss Snow beamed with pride. Xuân's easy victory, shameless showboating, and fancy racket and footwork gave him the glamorous aura of the privileged son of a famous Mandarin or a provincial governor. Victor Ban returned to investigate the commotion. Seeing the crowd go wild for the victor, he

1. Tennis.
2. Set.

decided that this Xuân could not be the same Xuân who had once worked for him.

After the game the loser congratulated Xuân and expressed his desire for a rematch at a later date. Overcome with pride, Miss Snow thought to herself that Xuân clearly deserved not only to be her boyfriend but to ruin her reputation as well. Hence, back in their room she was taken aback when he plopped down on the bed, utterly exhausted. She took a seat on the arm of a chair and sadly contemplated his impolite behavior. Suddenly, she heard the sound of a female voice singing from the adjacent room.

> Zè . . . đờ . . . đá . . . múa . . . !
> Mông pế y ề Pa rí! . . .[3]

"Oh, my darling! . . . Oh, Miss Snow!" Xuân called out, oblivious to the singing.

"Be quiet! My goodness . . . it's . . . it's . . . my sister! Sunset!"

"Oh, no!" Xuân cried out. "Who's that? Is it Mrs. Civilization?"

"No! Keep your voice down! It's my sister, the wife of the senior postal clerk!"

"Really? Is the horned senior clerk there, too?"

"How do you know about the horns?" Miss Snow asked in astonishment. "How? How did you find out that Sunset has a lover?"

"How could I not know?!" Xuân replied cleverly.

At that moment Mrs. Sunset, the wife of the horned senior clerk, and her lover were having an intimate conversation, unaware that Xuân and Snow were eavesdropping in the next room.

"Oh, my love," cooed Mrs. Sunset's lover, "we can't go on like this forever. It's too dangerous."

"What do you mean?" Mrs. Sunset asked angrily.

"I want you . . . I want us to get married!"

"You mean . . . you want me to divorce my husband?"

"What else could I mean?"

"But . . . I want you as a lover not a husband! Would you really want to be my husband? Then you would have horns, too! Isn't it better that he have horns instead of you?"

---

3. "J'ai deux amours, mon pays et Paris" (I have two loves, my country and Paris): a popular Josephine Baker song during the 1930s.

101

"Damn! What kind of woman has such a bizarre ideology?"

"What's so bizarre about it? Men may not understand it, but that's the way all women think today! To have only a husband and no lover is cowardly! Where is the virtue in that, the beauty, the intelligence? Not even a ghost would desire a woman like that! If I had no lover, my friends would scorn me! How could I show my face in public? I would barely be considered a real woman at all! A water buffalo is only a true water buffalo when it eats and fights. You should be happy that I am faithful to you and do not take a second lover."

"Then why aren't you faithful to your husband as well?"

"I am faithful to both of you! My husband and my lover! That's what makes me a woman."

"But, I'm afraid that he may find out one day . . ."

"Never! He was born with horns. Believe me, he'll never know. If the owl knew that he stank, then he would not stink anymore! . . . 'Zè đờ đá múa! Mông á măng, mông mà rrri!'"[4] She sang the rest of the song.

"What a virtuous woman!" Xuân whispered to Miss Snow. "How worthy! How fashionable!"

Xuân's praise for her older sister made Miss Snow jealous. "And I suppose you think that I—"

Xuân kissed Miss Snow passionately on the mouth. "You are also worthy!" he said in a sultry voice.

"My family is wealthy, sophisticated, and civilized," Miss Snow said, holding her head high. "My sister and I must be exactly alike in all things. It's the only way to maintain family decorum!"

Xuân hurriedly placed his hands on Miss Snow's breasts. This time, however, she pushed them away.

"You have done that already. Are you not yet satisfied that they are not made of rubber?"

But after Red-Haired Xuân offered a broad variety of suggestive comments, Miss Snow relaxed her resistance and remained silent, thus confirming the profound uncanniness of the fairer sex. They joked back and forth and eventually began uttering virtuous and deep-felt sentiments to each other.

---

4. "J'ai deux amours, mon amant, mon mari!" (I have two loves, my lover and my husband).

"Our love is a noble love . . ."

"Our love is a pure and soulful love."

Finally, Red-Haired Xuân brought up the ultimate favor.

"Quiet! Leave me alone!" Miss Snow stood up angrily. "I will never give you the ultimate favor! You are not a polite man! I am not as foolish as many innocent girls! I plan to remain a partially pure girl!"

Red-Haired Xuân was astounded.

"In other words, a *demi vierge!*"[5] she continued. "I will maintain half of my virginity!"

"Half of your virginity? A semi–virgin?"

"Of course!" Miss Snow replied haughtily. "How can I let my virginity be completely lost! Do you think I would risk the delivery of an earless roasted pig the day after my wedding?!"[6]

From then on Xuân was proper and well behaved. He understood that Miss Snow was a semi–virgin, an unusual kind of woman that our land of Nam can be proud to have produced here in the twentieth century.

---

5. Semi–virgin.

6. According to Vietnamese tradition, the bride's family must present the head of a pig to the groom's family prior to the wedding night. If the virginity of the bride is called into question, the groom's family returns the pig's head to the bride's family the following morning, after slicing off its ears.

Chapter 10

Red-Haired Xuân the Poet

❧

A Fight Over Horns

❧

The Conservatism of Mrs. Deputy
Customs Officer

After eating an elegant French meal in the dining room like the other upper-crust Vietnamese guests, Miss Snow suggested a walk in the Fairyland Hotel's garden. Fearing another encounter with Victor Ban, Xuân cited exhaustion and politely declined.

"That's odd," Miss Snow pouted. "You don't go to the Fairyland Hotel to be exhausted. You go to have fun! This is an era of science, physical fitness, and sports. How can you be exhausted? You are a healthy young man, a doctor no less! Are you telling the truth? I thought you loved women desperately like the French! It makes me wonder what might have happened had I allowed you to defile my honor."

Her ideas impressed Xuân, and he struggled for a response. "We are very honored to serve you."

He turned to leave, but Miss Snow stopped him. "What's the rush?!"

She began counting out loud to herself on her fingers. "One female friend, two male friends, Victor Ban—that's four people! There are now at least four people, my dear, who must suspect that I'm a bad girl. Isn't it wonderful? It will only be a matter of days until rumors reach my parents and that bastard of a fiancé. Sweet revenge will soon be mine!"

"The life of a horned husband is full of misery," Xuân said. "Nor is there much joy for a horned fiancé."

"How profound you are!" Miss Snow replied, laughing. "Your way of speaking is so characteristically twentieth century. But there's no need to worry. I could never plant horns on your head."

She paused for a moment. "You have never mentioned your parents before. How is the health of your *via* and the old woman of your house?"

"I was orphaned as a small child," Xuân answered sadly.

"Did you lose both of your parents, or is one still alive?"

"They both died."

Miss Snow's eyes lit up.

"That makes you an even better catch! If I marry you, I won't have a mother-in-law! What happiness! What a stroke of luck that you were orphaned early."

Xuân did not know how to respond.

"No need to worry, Doctor," she continued. "I'm not as reckless as other girls. I know how to protect myself."

"You will have to do it eventually . . ." Xuân replied impishly.

"Forget about it!" she said firmly. "I suppose you are looking forward to cutting off the ears of the roast pig on our wedding night?"

Her sharp response pleased Red-Haired Xuân and gave him hope that, if he were to marry Miss Snow in the future, he need not worry about sprouting horns.

Arm in arm, they walked outside together and into a garden that was as lush and colorful as a real fairyland. Lilies and snapdragons bloomed in the flower beds, and withered petals lay helter-skelter along the pebbled path. After several minutes they noticed that they were being followed by a short young man with glassy eyes, an emaciated body, and the gaunt face of a poet. He wore a European-style suit, and his pants were cuffed in the so-called elephant style. He stared anxiously at Miss Snow.

"Here! I'll show you someone who is desperate to win my heart . . ." she whispered to Xuân.

Xuân's face reddened with jealousy, and he turned around to look. Focusing intently on the object of his desire, the young man did not notice Xuân and continued to walk toward Miss Snow in his elephant cuffs.

"Ignore him, my dear!" Miss Snow said in a low voice. "He is just a poet! He can't do any harm."

Miss Snow grinned merrily as young girls often do when they are being pursued. She began hopping and skipping between the withered flowers along the pebbled path. The poet followed her. Just as Xuân was about to scold him for being impolite and presumptuous, the young man stopped and recited a poem aloud.

The fairy's feet were light as air.
Ashamed, young buds fell everywhere.
Beauty envies rival beauty.
She tramples flowers underfoot—alas.

Miss Snow giggled appreciatively, and Xuân's hatred gave way to a begrudging respect. Like poets everywhere, the young man did not flinch in the face of life's bitterness. Instead, he put on a brave face and recited another poem.

If not a bud beneath her feet,
My heart is sad, my gloom complete.
I pick a wilted flower up
To press against my throbbing heart! . . .

The poet stopped and bent down. He picked up a flower and pressed it tightly against his heart as if embracing an imaginary lover. No longer hearing the patter of footsteps behind her, Miss Snow glanced back over her shoulder. There she saw the poet hugging the flower with both arms.

"How moving!" she said. "That man has been following me for months. He loves me deeply, but I feel nothing for him!"

"Is he really in love with you?" asked Xuân between clenched teeth.

"What else would you call it?"

A number of literary possibilities ran through Xuân's mind. He felt compelled to compose a brief poem to compete with his new rival. How hard could it be? He recalled numerous jingles that he had recited flawlessly by heart in the past, back when he chanted advertisements over a loudspeaker for Victor Ban. "Would you like me to improvise a poem for that guy?"

Miss Snow clapped her hands with joy. "I would like nothing more," she squealed.

Placing his hands behind his back, Red-Haired Xuân approached the poet and began to versify in a loud and dignified voice:

No matter if you're young or old,
Avoid the sun, the wind, the cold.
Beware fevers, headaches, and the flu;
dry skin and heat rash make you blue.
Day and night you'll rant and rave.
Your feet won't walk, your hands won't wave.
For you I have these words to say:
Buy our ointment, don't delay.

Red-Haired Xuân wanted to continue, but the young man put up his hands to signal surrender.

"Forgive me, Sir!" he stammered. "Your humble student has learned his lesson . . . Your talent is truly great! I clearly must study the satirical poetic genres before I even dare attempt a response!"

Shamefaced, the poet bowed low to Xuân. Then he turned and scurried off.

"My goodness! What a talented man you are! Your poem was as scathingly satirical as Tú Mỡ's.[1] But why is your verse so full of medical terms?"

Stumped by the question, Xuân responded cleverly with one of his own. "Why do you think it is?"

Miss Snow then answered for herself: "Of course! You were a student at the medical college! That's why your poetry is so scientific. Right? Yours is the poetry of a man of medicine."

Xuân and Miss Snow strolled merrily over to the swimming pool. Suddenly, Miss Snow blanched. "Damn! It's the senior clerk! I've got to get out of here!"

She ducked behind a tree and disappeared.

Red-Haired Xuân spied the horned senior clerk walking together with a young woman. His beard was neatly trimmed, and he was dressed in an unusually elegant way. In spite of his horns, he looked uncharacteristically content, almost happy. His companion dressed

---

1. The pseudonym for a well-known satirical poet of the era.

in a style that was partially modern and partially old-fashioned. She looked like someone who embraced both the bad manners of a liberated woman and the old virtues of a traditional one. It was difficult to tell, in fact, which kind of woman she was!

Red-Haired Xuân was unsure if the woman was the senior clerk's wife. If not, then life was even more complicated than he had imagined. In any case Xuân quickly recalled his obligation to the senior clerk. After gesturing for the couple's attention, he bowed low, straightened himself up, and stuck out his chest.

"You, Sir, are a horned husband!" he announced in the booming voice of a human loudspeaker.

The senior clerk turned pale. "This, this is . . . my girlfriend, only!" he stammered.

"No kidding!" Xuân replied stupidly. "What a lucky coincidence! At this minute your wife is here in the hotel with her boyfriend. They are tending to your horns as we speak."

The senior clerk turned even paler. "What!?" he screamed hoarsely. "Right here in the Fairyland?"

"Where else could such a thing happen?" Xuân replied.

"Damn it! Take me to her now! Please! Let's go!"

Red-Haired Xuân immediately started to lead the way, eager to witness a love affair. Xuân stopped in front of the room and glanced at the horned senior clerk. The horned senior clerk took a deep breath and knocked at the door. After fifteen minutes the door cracked open. A high-pitched scream echoed from within the room.

"My God! My husband!"

"That bitch! That ill-bred dog!" the senior clerk scowled.

Red-Haired Xuân and the other woman stood by apprehensively. The hotel guests were busy swimming, diving, and bathing in the lake, oblivious to the tragic predicament of the senior clerk.

His wife's lover came to the door, fully dressed. "Greetings, Sir!" he said gently. "So, you are the husband?"

"Who the hell else would I be?" replied the senior clerk, fuming with anger.

His wife's lover bowed his head respectfully. His plan was to outmaneuver the senior clerk by demonstrating superior social skills.

"I am honored to make your acquaintance, Sir. Please try to keep in mind our exalted social positions. I am sure you will agree that it is important for us to maintain the utmost decorum."

The gambit seemed to produce the desired effect on the senior clerk.

"Yes, of course. In spite of my horns, I am still a refined, upper-class intellectual."

"I am glad you are being so sensible. I trust you will continue to maintain your level-headedness. After all, this is certainly not your first pair of horns. There is no reason to get angry. It will only make people laugh at us both. Indeed, I must tell you that, in spite of all that has happened, I still respect your wife deeply."

Ever conscious of their social reputations, the two men continued to address each other in extremely respectful tones. Eventually, however, the senior clerk began to break down.

"Sir, although my wife has put her clothes back on, I remain somewhat concerned. You must know the old saying: 'When a man visits a woman's room, he is absent-minded, but when a woman visits a man's room, she is a slut.'"

His wife's lover was impressed by the intellectual power of the senior clerk's reasoning. Sensing the impossibility of denying his adulterous crime, he tried a different approach.

"Sir, sprouting horns is not so bad. It is merely a question of bad luck, like an unintended accident. Take Napoléon, for example. Not only did he win great victories in the North and the East, but he was extremely handsome. And yet he too sprouted horns."

The comparison to Napoléon eased the mind of the horned senior clerk. But he continued to protest. "Whether it's my fault or not, there is no profit in sprouting horns. How do you plan to compensate me for the damage that you have inflicted? Perhaps I ought to seek recourse from the law?"

The idea of police or media involvement frightened the lover. He racked his brain for another solution. "Sir, it is I, in fact, who have sprouted horns!"

"Oh! Oh! Is that possible?" asked the senior clerk in disbelief.

"It is, indeed! Your wife told me that she was unmarried and considers me to be a sort of common-law husband. This is the first time I have heard of your existence. You have caught us red-handed, that is true. But, in point of fact, your wife has been enjoying two husbands simultaneously. Hence, I am also a horned husband. I too have been damaged. I also demand compensation!"

"I don't know what you are talking about! Mr. Xuân, will you please confirm to this man that I am the horned husband?"

Xuân bowed his head. "We are honored to serve you," he replied courteously.

"It is unclear who has damaged whom," the lover added threateningly. "Perhaps I should consult my lawyer about this matter. As an office clerk, you are no doubt familiar with the law. And the law must be respected!"

Upon hearing the word *lawyer*, the senior clerk began worrying about the legality of his own presence in the Fairyland Hotel. He feared that his reputation as a model official might be tarnished. Perhaps it was he who would be caught red-handed during his attempt to catch his wife and her lover red-handed. With these thoughts in mind, he winked at his own lover and extended his hand to his wife's.

"Farewell, Sir! I hope to see you again . . ."

Like an escaped convict, he dashed out the front gate of the Fairyland Hotel, followed by his lover. Xuân was also struck by the reference to lawyers. Fearing dire repercussions, he walked swiftly away without looking back.

He quickly came upon Miss Snow. "We must leave immediately," he said to her. "Otherwise, there will be trouble!"

Frightened and flustered, Miss Snow followed Xuân to the Japanese gate. As they passed through it, the car of Mrs. Deputy Customs Officer pulled up in front of the hotel.

Mrs. Deputy Customs Officer jumped out of the car and called out the name of Miss Snow. "You are engaged already, my dear. Your presence here calls into question the high moral standards of your family!"

Miss Snow pointed at Xuân. "We're just friends! No more, no less."

Miss Snow flagged a rickshaw. She got in and took off down the street, leaving Xuân and Mrs. Deputy Customs Officer behind.

"Young girls today are so ill bred. They do nothing but eat and go out on the town. A woman's duty is to follow and remain faithful to her husband. Whatever happened to the three obligations and the four virtues? Whatever happened to chastity, morality, and decorum?"

Xuân stood there, his mouth shut tightly like a mussel.

"And you, Mr. Xuân. You must behave yourself. Don't ruin other people's lives. She is engaged, meaning she is taken already. Remember the saying: 'Chase only unmarried men or widows; do not pursue the husbands and wives of other people!'"

This brief lecture in morality reminded Xuân of his earlier problems. It also reminded him that Mrs. Deputy Customs Officer was, in fact, a widow.

"Madame, please forgive me," he stammered. "If you were not so famously faithful to your two ex-husbands . . . I would certainly have pursued you, instead!"

Mrs. Deputy Customs Officer smiled. "Oh, how naughty of you to say so!"

She hopped back into her car and sped off, a fugitive from love.

Red-Haired Xuân bade farewell to the Fairyland Hotel and returned to the Europeanization Tailor Shop on foot.

Chapter 11

Opening Day at the Tennis Court
❧

Red-Haired Xuân: Master Orator
❧

Preparations for a Marriage

The opening of Mrs. Deputy Customs Officer's private tennis court was truly a historic event for sports in Vietnam. As with most opening days, this one included a tea party, champagne toasts, and a formal speech.

Present at the party were Mr. ILL and his wife, Miss Snow and her two older siblings (the high school graduate and Mrs. Sunset, the wife of the horned senior clerk), and the royalist politician Joseph Thiết.

Sitting amid the huge crowd, Joseph Thiết imagined that he was a great political leader surrounded by the masses on all sides. Like a true political leader, Joseph Thiết was deeply concerned about the good of the nation while simultaneously despising the tastes and amusements of the masses. Ignoring the noisy din of the crowd, he opened a French newspaper and read the agreeable news that a disciple of the royalist Maurras had recently bloodied the face of M. Léon Blum. He experienced a momentary sensation that there was no one in the crowd but himself. The crowd ignored him as well.

Other than little Master Blessing (No way!), everyone who was anyone in high society came out for the event. The crowd grew more and more tipsy, and the upper crust sank lower and lower. Mr.

Civilization, frail and supremely unathletic, stood up and raised his glass. "Ladies and Gentlemen."

Mr. Civilization rattled on for almost an hour. He spoke about the tradition of sports in ancient Greece, about our own national sporting movement, and about the crucial importance of sports for the future of the race. He recounted the biography of Mrs. Senior Clerk (otherwise known as Mrs. Deputy Customs Officer) and praised her fashionable and progressive vision of building a tennis court to promote the cause of sports within her family. He went on to sing the praises of female athletes, singling out Miss Junior Walking Race. He also attacked "old fuddy-duddies" who waste all their money building village communal houses, restoring old Buddhist statues and pagodas, or casting bronze temple bells.

He allowed that the traditional practice of spirit possession might be considered a kind of sport, although a rather dated one.

The journalist who advocated progressive reforms for society at large and conservative practices for his own family scribbled down the great man's valuable ideas.

Mr. Civilization then outlined the qualities characteristic of the ideal woman so that Mrs. Deputy Customs Officer could be sure that she was one. He concluded by introducing Red-Haired Xuân: an exemplary young man and professor of tennis who had received virtually every honor that someone in his position might possibly acquire. In short, the speech possessed all the necessary attributes of a formal oratorical address by a great man of letters or an important politician: embellishment, fabrication, exaggeration, fantasy, and duplicity—all dressed up in the dishonest language of literature. The crowd applauded enthusiastically.

Upon the conclusion of his speech, Mr. Civilization took his seat in a dignified and falsely modest fashion—as all public announcers tend to do. His aunt rose to respond. Mrs. Deputy Customs Officer thanked the announcer and all the ladies and gentlemen who had turned out for the opening day ceremonies of her new tennis court. She expressed the hope that it would always be so crowded.

Everyone clapped again . . .

Unfamiliar with the rituals of opening day ceremonies and distracted by the attention bestowed upon him, Red-Haired Xuân did not realize that he was expected to respond publicly. Instead, he nursed a tall glass of champagne and applauded loudly with the rest of the crowd. Even as members of the crowd began glancing at him expectantly, he folded his arms and remained silent. His ungrateful attitude provoked murmurs of disapproval from the crowd. Finally, the wife of the horned senior clerk stood up and addressed him. "Now it is time for a few words from Mr. Xuân, the tennis professor."

Eager for any opportunity to needle Xuân, Mr. ILL urged him on as well. "That is right! Every honor should rain down upon the tennis professor on this, the opening day of the tennis court! Please, Sir, put your modesty aside. Honor us with your words of wisdom."

"Go ahead, Doctor!" chimed in Miss Snow. "Say something clever! Show them how it's done!"

Like a mechanical puppet manipulated by a team of puppet masters, Red-Haired Xuân stood up, still holding his champagne. A speech? He had never before been shy about speaking loudly in public, and he never lost his voice, two important qualities for a good orator. In the past he had always been extremely effective using his voice to conquer, oppress, and move the hearts of the masses—whether selling roasted peanuts, working as an advertising boy at the theater, or making loudspeaker announcements for the Cochinchinese King of Venereal Disease Treatment.

Speaking was not the problem. The problem was: what to say . . . ?

He thought deeply for several minutes. Gradually, his mind recalled the language often used by the Civilizations and Mr. ILL. He had grown accustomed to this language ever since the day he began shouldering the responsibility of Europeanizing society. As he began to speak, his mind raced forward searching for what to say next. "My dear girlfriends and boyfriends . . ."

Xuân based this unusual opening on something he had overheard at the Fairyland Hotel when he was trying to dishonor the respectable Miss Snow. The result was unexpectedly encouraging. Never before had the members of the audience been addressed by a public orator in such an intimate way. They listened in rapt attention.

"I have played a role in the movement for social reform . . . Still, I must work very hard and understand exactly what I am doing . . . We are still not Europeanized enough! . . . A roadblock on the road of evolution. Sports . . . Race . . . What is family happiness if not the happiness of husbands and their wives? We must all make an effort to exercise . . . We do not only reform the outside like those old fashioned moralists in the past . . . During this deeply reformist era, everything conservative will be eliminated! . . . We are honored to serve you."

Recalling the slogans typically shouted out when sports champions were awarded their trophies from high-ranking ministers or governors, Xuân concluded his speech. *Líp, líp, lơ . . .* Hua rra!"[1]

Just then, Joseph Thiết read in his newspaper that royalist newspapers were calling for the head of the socialist Léon Blum. Joseph Thiết, originally a member of the Thập tự Lửa Party, slapped his thighs and yelled out approvingly: "Bravo! Bravo!"

Following his lead, the crowd broke into thunderous applause. Mrs. Deputy Customs Officer issued a loud *Líp líp lơ.* Several skeptics in the crowd applauded as well but only because Red-Haired Xuân had delivered his own extemporaneous speech instead of relying on a prerecorded gramophone announcement, like most real athletes.

A round of champagne toasts followed during which people flattered each other like prime ministers at a summit. Then everyone descended to the tennis court.

A moving sight awaited their arrival. What a great moment for sports in this country and for the future of women! On the net of the tennis court, as brand new as a virgin girl, they saw one . . . two . . . three . . . four . . . panties, slips, underwear, trousers, and pajama bottoms, all made from silk, some embroidered, some made from lace. The panties, all of which belonged to Mrs. Deputy Customs Officer, were so stylish that even very old men began to get excited!

Mrs. Deputy Customs Officer was furious and scolded the laundry woman.

"Who could have known!" the old-fashioned laundress complained. "It looked like a good place to hang laundry!"

The items were removed and the tennis court was restored to its rightful function. For the first match Xuân played Mrs. Civilization. Then he went against Dr. Straight Talk. Finally, he teamed up with Dr. Straight Talk to play against Mrs. Civilization and an old friend of Mrs. Deputy Customs Officer who had married a Frenchman.

Meanwhile, at Grandpa Hồng's house rumors were flying that

---

1. Hip, hip, hip . . . Houra!

Miss Snow had been seen with Mr. Xuân. When she heard the news, Grandma gritted her teeth like an old-fashioned mother. "Will you never learn? Spoiling your children like that! When her belly swells up like a barrel . . . then you will understand the true meaning of Women's Rights, Civilization, Ultra Modernity, and Liberation! Remember the old saying, 'Children are spoiled by their mothers, grandchildren by their grandmothers!' Because you ruined her, because you spoiled her—now I will be cursed and criticized!"

To Grandpa, Grandma's conservative theories represented a major obstacle for the women's liberation movement in the country. He shut his eyes tightly. "I know! I know! What a pain! Shut up, already!"

Ignoring Grandpa's protest, Grandma ordered the opium servant into the kitchen. As a civilized man and a supporter of women's rights, Grandpa Hồng did not protest this attack on his servant. He lay yawning beside his opium tray as Grandma rattled on.

"Did you know that Xuân and Snow rented an *ô-ten*[2] room together?! Can you imagine . . . ?"

"I know! What a pain! Shut up, already!"

"Who would have suspected such behavior from Mr. Xuân? He seems so proper and well behaved, yet he turns out to be such a cad!"

"I know! What a pain! Shut up, already!"

Grandma suddenly imagined the things that men and women typically do together in a hotel room. She burst into tears like an old-fashioned mother. Hearing Grandma's cries, Grandpa opened his eyes. "What else, Grandma?"

Grandma cried even louder. "What else? What else can there be?!"

"You're so very old-fashioned, it's impossible to talk to you!"

"What is old-fashioned? Answer me that! If I may be so bold as to ask—what the hell is old-fashioned?"

"Nowadays, men and women are not segregated as in the era of our parents! Nowadays, men and women are free to be friends and to go out together for fun just like French people! Girls can have boyfriends just as they can have girlfriends. There is nothing unusual about it!"

"Who told you that?"

2. Hotel.

116

"My son!"

"And are you sure it's such a good thing?"

"Lúy[3] has assured me that it is. Even if he's wrong, what's the difference?"

"Your son! What a show-off! He opened that naughty tailor shop and now is involved in all kinds of monkey business! It's disgusting! I can't bear it anymore! Just because I never said anything doesn't mean I ever approved!"

"Who cares if it's disgusting? I only know that his Europeanization Tailor Shop brings in hundreds of piasters each month!"

"I'll tell you something else! Your daughter-in-law is now wearing shorts in front of me, her own husband's mother! How do you like that! You won't be so easygoing when it's your own daughter who gets into trouble!"

"How do you know she's pregnant? It's not always that easy!"

"Do you know what they did together? They bathed, they swam, and they danced! They rented a room together for a whole day!"

A half-hour had elapsed since the dismissal of the opium servant. Like a proper opium addict, Grandpa's eyes glazed over, and his nose began to run. He shut his eyes tightly. "I know! What a pain! Shut up, already!"

"Everyone knows that the two of them closed the door to their room and took a nap together. Did you know that?"

"So what? What else did they do?"

A look of pain crossed Grandma's face. "What do you think?!"

"How do you know? Who told you?"

"Her older sister!"

"Why was Sunset at the Fairyland?"

"Because her husband went there, that's why!"

"Quick! Call the servant to prepare opium for me! Enough of this story! Stop making such a fuss!"

But Grandma did not call the servant. Ignoring Grandpa's sacred rights as an opium addict, she continued to castigate him. "Do you think we should wait until her belly swells up like a barrel before making a fuss? Doesn't it bother you that Snow is already engaged? That bastard Xuân is a no-good, cheating dog! He's not a real man! Just you wait! I will force Civilization and that wife of his to fire him!

---

3. *Lui* (he).

I'll talk to Mrs. Deputy Customs Officer as well, that shameless old bitch! A tennis court? What a whore! I forbid that bastard Xuân to come over here ever again!"

"I know! What a pain! Shut up, already!"

"Mark my words, I will beat Snow to death! I will curse that bitch Deputy Customs Officer, you wait and see! . . . I will send Civilization's wife back to her mother! How do you like that, Mr. Progressive Civilization?"

"What a pain! Shut up, already! Call the servant to prepare my opium! Enough of this nonsense!"

Grandma slammed her fist down on the table. "I will not call him! You wait just a minute! Once you smoke your opium—it will be 'I know, I know' again and again!"

Grandpa sat up. "How dare you? You wait and see! I will marry Snow to Xuân. I promise! He used to be a student from the medical college, and now people call him doctor! Who knows, maybe he will win a tennis championship some day! Our family will be blessed for seventy generations if Snow gets pregnant by Xuân. Now be quiet and stop acting so stupid!"

Like all opium addicts, Grandpa became short-tempered when he needed a fix.

Chapter 12

The Peculiar Language of the
Old and the New
☞
A Princess Pricked by a Thorn
☞
The Irony of Fate

The alarm clock rang at eight in the morning. Mr. Civilization kicked off his blankets and sat up in bed. His lovable wife was nowhere to be seen. Glancing at the calendar on the wall, he suddenly remembered that today was Thursday, the day of her tennis lesson.

After washing his face and changing clothes, he buzzed for the servant, who appeared with a tray of milk cakes, butter, coffee, and chocolate—the favorite breakfast of upper-class intellectuals. He sat down at his wife's dressing table. As Mr. Civilization wolfed down the food, he combed his hair and began to make up his face. He painted his fingernails with bright-red nail polish. Then he applied pancake to his cheeks and covered them with a layer of powder. After toweling his face clean, he dabbed on another clownish layer of powder. With his black hair curling down the nape of his long neck, his bulging eyes and Adam's apple, and his milky white face, he looked like a feminine man of lipstick and powder . . .

Suddenly, he heard footsteps out in the hall approaching his room. The door swung open. Before he could curse the stupidity of the people of Annam for failing to knock before entering a room, he recognized that this particular Annamese offender was his own mother. He forced a smile and began wiping off his fashionable face. "What brings you here so early, Mother?"

Without answering the question, she placed her hands behind her back and peered around the room. A rolled cigarette dangled from the corner of her lips. Eventually, she sat down on the bed. "Where is she?" she asked.

"My wife is at the tennis court," he replied nervously. She shook her head disapprovingly. "What time did she leave?"

"Probably around seven this morning."

"Oh! What a civilized couple you are!"

He sensed what was coming: another episode in the never-ending conflict that split all families down the middle, the clash between the old and the new.

"If you say so, Mother," he replied.

The old woman was furious, but she tried to control herself. "Why aren't you at the shop? It's late! You will go bankrupt if you continue to be so lazy! With you sleeping late at home and your wife away, your employees will steal all of your money!"

Civilization continued to powder his face. "Mr. ILL is looking after the place, Mother."

Although she did not actually understand his response, she saw no point in pursuing this line of questioning further. The purpose of her visit, after all, was to raise the delicate question of Red-Haired Xuân.

"So, where is Dr. Xuân?" she asked.

"You mean the tennis professor? He is at the tennis court, no doubt."

Mr. Civilization had been misrepresenting Xuân's background for so long that he had almost come to believe the lies himself. In a matter of weeks he had succeeded in transforming Xuân from a ball boy into a professor. Once he had already presented Xuân as a progressive and highly educated medical student, it could never be admitted that he was actually a ball boy from a tennis club.

"I hear that you are going to allow Snow to take tennis lessons," Grandma asked. "Is that true?"

The question surprised him. "I don't even know if she is interested. I approve, of course. Tennis is very healthy. It can't do any harm."

"Mr. Xuân seems very proper and well behaved. Don't you think so . . . ?"

"Obviously!" he responded, unaware of his mother's machinations. "After all, did he not cure Great-Grandpa? We must be forever grateful to him for that. It is also thanks to him that business has been so good at the tailor shop!"

"But do you really think that Mr. Xuân is proper and well behaved?"

"No question about it. It is as clear as two plus two makes four."

She paused for a moment. "What would you think if we were to marry him to Snow? Would Xuân agree?"

This question made Mr. Civilization uneasy, and he frowned. "Why do you bring it up?" he replied cautiously.

"With a grown-up daughter, it is only natural to think about a son-in-law. It is the duty of parents to make sure that their children get married. Of course, you are aware of that."

Mr. Civilization shook his head. "I do not think that it would work out . . ."

"Damn!" she said, feigning disappointment. "Why not?"

"They do not come from families of the same social rank!" he answered, sounding like an old-fashioned moralist. "Plus, who knows if Mr. Xuân would agree to marry Snow . . . ?"

"I am afraid that it would be a shame for us if he refused. Anyway, I thought questions of social rank were unimportant to you . . . Aren't you always prattling on about . . . the common people?"

"Why are you so interested in this now, Mother?" he snapped.

"Because Mr. Xuân is proper and well behaved . . ."

"That's not enough! There must be something else!"

Grandma stood up, approached her son, and stuck a finger in his face. "There is something else. Mr. Xuân has slept with your younger sister already! You bastard!"

The old woman was overcome by a fit of dizziness. She reached unsteadily for the wall. "It's all your fault!" she moaned. "You let the bee live up your sleeve! Now everything is so complicated. You've ruined your little sister's life. You've sullied the family's honor. And what about those dirty rumors about him and your wife! Think of the stories people will tell!"

His mother's words struck Civilization like a thunderbolt. He was overcome by an urge to reject progressivism and return to the comforts of conservatism. Her reference to his wife inflamed his jealousy. Nothing frightened him as much as sprouting horns, despite the fact that horns were more a sign of progress than conservatism. Modern women who were virtuous were not a problem. Modern women who were not virtuous were also not a problem, especially for men who thought of women as toys . . . A problem only occurred when those toys were one's own sister and wife . . . No . . . It could never happen. "Are you sure about this? Were there witnesses?"

"Her older sister, the senior clerk's wife, saw them renting a room in the Fairyland Hotel. What more evidence do we need?"

"How strange! Why didn't she try to stop her younger sister? Why didn't she tell me?"

"She said she was too ashamed to say or do anything!"

"What does she have to be ashamed of?!"

"She said that she feared Snow would hate her and there would be a conflict between sisters. You shouldn't let Snow know that it was her older sister who told on her . . ."

Mr. Civilization thought for a while. "Let me check out the story to make sure that it is true. Then we will figure out what to do. Don't worry, Mother. Whatever's happened has happened. We must not panic."

Mr. Civilization sprayed perfume on his hair, grabbed his velvet hat, and raced down the stairs. Then he took off in search of Red-Haired Xuân.

The tennis court was empty except for Mrs. Civilization and Red-Haired Xuân. Miss Jannette, Mrs. Deputy Customs Officer's daughter, was home from school visiting her mother. She was seated courtside, with an open book between her knees. Her attention drifted back and forth from the action on the court to the pictures in her book. A couple of poorly dressed ten-year-old ball boys ran back and forth retrieving balls for Red-Haired Xuân, now a very well-dressed professor in Western-style pants, a sleeveless shirt, and a pair of white canvas tennis shoes.

Instead of running around the court in tennis shorts, practicing her backhand, as she had during the previous weeks, Mrs. Deputy Customs Officer remained upstairs. Her practice regimen had been interrupted by another sacred task—the task of a gentle mother. For some unknown reason, in the last two days little Master Blessing had eaten one less bowl of rice than usual. He would sit, quiet as a philosopher, for long stretches at a time without disturbing his nanny. He even stopped saying "No way!" What was happening to this boy blessed by Heaven and Buddha? The previous afternoon little Master Blessing had sneezed three times. That evening he got the hiccups after drinking a glass of water. During the night he wet his bed only once instead of twice as was customary. Early this morning he had coughed three times. What a bad omen! Although she revealed her fears to no one, Mrs. Deputy Customs Officer worried that something was terribly wrong.

Is it possible that little Master Blessing was going "to depart"?

Perhaps the Buddha from the Perfume Pagoda had fallen deeply in love with his own offspring,—who knew if the Buddha had children of his own? Perhaps the Buddha longed to release his child from the misery of earthly existence.

The fortune-teller had predicted that little Master Blessing was to live a long life. Could he be wrong?

Such questions preoccupied Master Blessing's mother and made her miserable with worry. If all parents are obsessed with the welfare of their children, imagine the anxiety of a mother with a child sent directly from Heaven. She had carefully avoided all taboo food and activities thought to bring bad luck and had refrained from offering praise for her son that might draw the attention of evil spirits. She had made offerings and pledged to dedicate her son to Heaven. She had carried an incense bowl on her head and chanted verse written in Chinese characters. She had prayed. There was nothing that she had not done. And still "this" had happened! She contemplated calling upon the famous monk Brother Tăng Phú or consulting with Dr. Straight Talk. As she stared desperately at little Master Blessing sitting atop a table in the middle of the room, her gaze fixated upon the tennis players through the upstairs window. While respecting and admiring them, she was struck by their callousness in the face of her son's predicament. Her anger dissipated quickly, however, after she remembered that she had not yet informed anyone of the news, not even her maids and servants. She feared that disclosure might, somehow, bring bad luck . . . What a mess!

At that moment Mr. Civilization pushed open the gate and walked into the yard. He tipped his hat to Miss Jannette and stopped briefly to chat with her. Spying his wife over her shoulder, he was struck by the fact that her shorts were too short and revealed too much of her shapely, white legs. This was especially troubling given her proximity to such a suspicious character as Red-Haired Xuân.

For a moment the very idea of progressive social reform repelled him. At the very least, he thought, his wife's shorts could do with a little more conservatism. The sight of Xuân concentrating feverishly on the game, however, eased his mind a little.

"Enough! How about a short break?" he shouted. "My dear! I would like to speak with you in private."

She tapped her racket on the ground three times to signal a time-out and headed toward her husband.

"Please excuse us for a minute," Mr. Civilization said politely to Xuân.

"No problem," replied Xuân, gasping for breath.

The couple walked leisurely toward the gate.

"Do you know what has happened?" the husband asked.

His tone frightened her, and she opened her eyes wide. "What? What's going on?"

The husband shook his head. "We cannot allow Xuân into our house ever again! He is a complete bastard!"

"How come? Business is very good and most of our customers belong to him. Besides, who will practice with me? I need to prepare for the emperor's visit. Why are you so down on him, anyway?"

"He and our Snow have become entangled."

"Really? Yes, you are probably right. I suspected as much!"

"According to what I've heard, they may have slept together already."

"Damn it! Really? Are you sure?"

"I want to bash the face of that son-of-a-bitch! You know that we will be blamed for our sister's behavior. My mother already said that it is our fault for being so progressive and Europeanized. She blames us for spoiling Snow. Can you believe it?"

"Mother knows about it? What did she say?"

"Mom and Dad want Snow to marry that bastard. Isn't that disgraceful?"

"Oh no! Why rush into things? We must find out exactly what happened!"

"How can we find out? We can't force her to be examined by a doctor. And, if it is true, she would never dare tell us."

"You are right. She probably loves him and wants to marry him. She also knows that—if the worst has happened already—our parents must consent to a wedding. She may even try to exaggerate what they have done, just to get what she wants."

"Yes. Or maybe they have not slept together yet, but, because they want to force our hand, they will arrange a quickie. Who knows?"

"So, why did you plan to bash Xuân's face?"

"I was too angry to think straight! But wait . . . there may be a solution. First, we must make sure that they stay apart for the time being. Then we can try to find out if that bastard Xuân has ruined her yet. Once we know one way or the other, we can then decide what to do—either marry our younger sister to him or lock her up."

"The first step is to kick that bastard Xuân out of the tailor shop and forbid him to return. It will mean sacrificing a valuable employee."

"It also means that we will sacrifice a great social reformer for the good of our old-fashioned family!"

"That's right! But, remember, it's our sacrifice that counts."

"Maybe I should tell Auntie Senior Clerk to ask him to stay here with her."

"Great idea! But don't be too obvious about it."

As the couple returned to the tennis court, they saw the Frenchman's wife waving desperately from the corner window on the second floor. Imagining the worst, they ran into the house, dashed up the stairs, and entered the room. It seemed that little Master Blessing had sneezed four times in a row! Mr. Civilization comforted his aunt by offering a handful of vague physiological explanations for the extra sneeze. After she had calmed down, he sat down to contemplate the problem of Red-Haired Xuân.

Hence, Xuân's efforts to ruin innocent Miss Snow's reputation had been a complete success.

Before him lay a greater challenge: how to destroy the reputation of a widow who was utterly faithful to her two husbands.

Chapter 13

A Physiological Investigation

━

The Language of an Authentic Monk

━

Red-Haired Xuân Reforms Buddhism

While Dr. Straight Talk examined little Master Blessing on the second floor, Xuân remained downstairs in the servants' quarters. The household staff was puzzled by his mysterious class background and social rank, but they knew that their mistress looked up to Xuân, and so they too treated him with respect. Indeed, Xuân's easygoing manner put them at ease. They liked the fact that he was unpretentious and spoke the language of the common people; he often used popular phrases such as "Damn it!" and "God-damn my mother's milk."

As with household employees everywhere, the maids and servants spent their free time bad-mouthing their employers and exchanging gossip about the foibles of the high and mighty.

"Rich people are so strange!" the driver said. "They make such a huge fuss over nothing! She acts like the kid is going to croak, but there's absolutely nothing wrong with him! What's the big deal? Can you believe that they actually called a doctor? God only knows what will become of that kid!"

Master Blessing's nanny joined in the class struggle.

"What about children from poor families! They don't even have enough food to eat, and still they are not as sickly as that brat! When they do come down with something, they find a way to cure themselves!"

The cook was even more harsh. He put forth the theory that the boy was, in fact, an ordinary human being and not a gift from Heaven or Buddha. He suggested that the onset of puberty combined with an overly rich diet had induced changes in the boy's blood and general constitution. He was merely experiencing extreme growing pains, a function of his remarkably precocious physical development.

"Just take a look at him," he insisted. "Have you noticed how he pretends to suckle Nanny's breast, just to cop a quick feel. 'No way' indeed! He's just horny, like his mother. How about when he forces Nanny to play horse so that he can mount her from behind. Give me a break! Like mother, like son, if you ask me . . ."

"That's what I call a God-damned gift from Heaven!" said Xuân sternly.

To save face the nanny tried to make an excuse for little Master Blessing. "It's not true. He's just a little boy. He doesn't know what he's doing."

"I know what the hell he's doing," the driver interjected. "I've seen lots of children in my life. Kids today become perverts much earlier than in the old days! Some even take lovers and go to brothels! Even if he doesn't know what he's doing, he's gonna have to marry someone soon if he keeps it up! How can he not be a pervert with a depraved mother like that? He's not listless because he's going to die — he's probably just thinking up really dirty thoughts. Being a gift from Heaven has nothing to do with it . . ."

After expressing support for the driver's analysis, Xuân went upstairs to consult with Dr. Straight Talk. When he entered the room, the doctor and the gentle mother were standing nervously in front of the naked boy, who was refusing to put his clothes on. The doctor was stumped. Despite his mother's insistence that the boy was ill, he could find nothing wrong with the child.

"Maybe he's right," said Mr. Civilization. "Maybe little Master Blessing is not really sick."

This suggestion upset Mrs. Deputy Customs Officer; she was afraid that it might bring bad luck to say such a thing out loud.

"Indeed!" Dr. Straight Talk agreed. "It is probably nothing more than the onset of puberty. If you were to find him a wife—"

"You are correct Sir," Xuân butted in. "I have known many of today's children."

Dr. Straight Talk extended his hand to Xuân as if meeting an old confidant. Encouraged by Xuân's support, he began to pontificate on various indelicate subjects. "Of course, of course! I am sure that my esteemed colleague here is familiar with the theories of Freud. Yes? Symptoms of the nervous system indicate problems with the kidneys and can give rise to a host of peculiar conditions . . ."

While Dr. Straight Talk's erudition surprised no one, Xuân's was unexpected.

"We understand each other like brothers," Xuân responded. "No need to explain."

Mrs. Deputy Customs Officer could not follow Dr. Straight Talk's diagnosis, but she understood enough to be annoyed that it failed to highlight the fact that her son was a gift from Heaven and Buddha. She sensed, however, that she was outnumbered and remained silent. Red-Haired Xuân signaled to Dr. Straight Talk that he wished to consult with him in private. They moved over to the window.

"Although I am not the primary physician, I am quite familiar with the boy and his condition. As a colleague, Sir, I feel it is my duty to inform you that the boy is entering puberty. He often forces his nanny to let him suckle her breasts like some sort of three-year-old. But, in fact, he's just horny!"

Dr. Straight Talk put his forefinger to his lips and nodded in agreement.

"Thank you very much, Sir! You have identified the physiological crux of the matter. There is no avoiding the truth. Once again, Freud provides the solution. The boy is exhibiting signs of early puberty brought on by too much rich food, too many nice clothes, and excessive pampering of the body. These factors combine to enhance his lechery. The problem is exacerbated by the particular environment in which he lives. Wouldn't you agree, Sir?"

Xuân stared at the window. His ears had grown bored listening to all the unfamiliar words, and eventually they stopped paying attention. At that moment several animals in the garden were engaging in the joys of procreation. There were a pair of doves coupling on the roof and two pretty Japanese dogs circling each other hungrily down in the yard. In the garden a rooster was mounting a hen. As fate would have it, all these domestic animals were demonstrating the miraculous logic of Yin and Yang simultaneously. Distracted by the raunchy spectacle, Xuân ignored the doctor's question.

"Don't you think we ought to consider the significance of the surrounding environment?" the doctor asked again.

"The surrounding environment?" Xuân responded in a dazed stupor. "What surrounding environment?"

Dr. Straight Talk turned to see what Xuân was staring at. Seeing the animal love fest, he grabbed Xuân's hand once again and shook it vigorously. "My dear . . . dear friend! Once again you have put your finger on an obscure but important factor influencing human behavior. The evidence to which you allude supports our theory. Of course, it is very dangerous for adolescents to be exposed to such filth firsthand."

"We must change the surrounding environment immediately!" said Xuân.

Dr. Straight Talk cleared his throat and, true to his name, announced the diagnosis in a direct and dignified manner. "Indeed! There is nothing else to say! My good friend and I have reached the same conclusion. Mankind's greatest weakness has always been lust! When a newborn baby suckles and caresses his mother's breasts, lust is born! When a ten-year-old boy reaches puberty—"

"In spite of the fact that he is clearly a gift sent from Heaven and Buddha," interrupted Xuân, "he is as susceptible to lust as any normal person. He may even be more lustful!"

"There is no need for a cure because the boy is not sick!" the doctor chimed in. "What he needs is to get married. If you're afraid that it's too early, you must begin to prepare him . . . to educate him. This will not be an easy task; it will take much care and patience. But, if you have someone like my good friend here to help, it can certainly be done."

"Auntie," said Mrs. Civilization, seizing the opportunity, "why don't you ask Mr. Xuân to stay here and educate little Master Blessing. He will protect the boy from the unhealthy surrounding environment."

"We will do whatever the doctor orders," replied Mrs. Deputy Customs Officer. "I will order a private room prepared for Mr. Xuân."

The Civilizations left together with Dr. Straight Talk. Dr. Red-Haired Xuân stayed behind. With her mind at ease, Mrs. Deputy Customs Officer issued a flurry of orders to the servants and retired to her room. In the living room Red-Haired Xuân paced back and forth, thinking to himself. Suddenly, he heard a voice ring out from the hallway.

"Is anyone home?! *Amitabha!* Greetings, sir!"

When he turned around, Red-Haired Xuân found himself face to face with a fashionable, modern, and surprisingly Europeanized monk. He wore a dyed brown shirt made from Shanghai silk and a pair of sandals with rubber heels. In his mouth Xuân noticed three gold teeth. He was handsome and had an almost sensual look about him.

"What can I do for you?" asked Red-Haired Xuân. "Please take a seat!"

"With your permission . . . Sir, I am a poor monk who lives but an ascetic and onerous existence. In addition, I am the publisher of a newspaper called the *Wooden Fish Drum*. Amitabha!"

"The *Wooden Fish Drum?*" said Xuân in an amused voice. "Does it educate the public about the proper kind of drumbeat to be played when entertaining singing girls?"

The monk blushed. "Sir, a singing girl can also contribute to the enlightenment of the spirit, as it is written in the Confucian Book of Music. Monks who visit singing girls do not necessarily abandon asceticism. Their musical diet remains strictly meatless, if you know what I mean. They never stay overnight. You may recall the recent case in which I, a poor monk, successfully sued a newspaper editor who accused me of lewd behavior in a house of ill repute. Even the laws of the Protectorate Government side with poor monks in these matters!"

"No kidding? Really? That's terrific!"

"As you can see, although I am only a poor monk, I am not without power. The *Wooden Fish Drum* counts among its patrons many high mandarins, governors-general, residents superior, and military officials. We have hung their giant portraits all over the offices of our newspaper . . . Ah, Buddhism is so mysterious—so deep and so lofty."

"How can a bunch of ascetic monks run a commercially competitive newspaper?" asked Red-Haired Xuân, zeroing in on a knotty Buddhist dilemma.

"There is a good explanation," the monk replied. "You have heard perhaps that a new Buddhist Association with its own newspaper has been founded in our country. We were afraid that it would cut into the popularity of our pagoda. Hence, we poor monks decided to publish the *Wooden Fish Drum* in order to protect ourselves from the competition."

With one mystery of Buddhism cleared up, Red-Haired Xuân turned to another.

"So, you mean that monks today promote themselves and compete with each other just like rival Kings of Venereal Disease Treatment!"

"Amitabha!" the monk responded enthusiastically. "As a matter of fact, one King of Venereal Disease Treatment sits on the editorial board of the *Wooden Fish Drum!* He has helped us to develop an aggressive and broad-based advertising strategy. Do not think that, just because we are monks, we do not know anything about journalism or pen wars! Secular journalists attack each other in print as stupid, uneducated, and untalented, but we Buddhist journalists are not afraid to expose the fact that our enemies are stricken with scabies, herpes, leprosy, or loss of a major limb!"

"Wow!" said Xuân. "That must be great for your circulation!"

"It certainly is! Since I started the *Wooden Fish Drum*, our following has expanded. The quantity of paper goods and money burned at our alters is way up, as is the number of people who worship at our pagoda. We have also seen significant growth in coffin donations and the number of children consecrated by their parents. It is my sacred duty as a monk to support the development of Buddhism. Our success in the face of such aggressive tactics by the new Buddhist Association testifies to the Buddha's support for our efforts . . ."

Red-Haired Xuân stood up and interrupted the monk.

"But why are you here, Brother? What do you want from us? I am not going to buy the *Wooden Fish Drum*. I prefer the kind of drum that you monks beat when you take in one of your so-called meatless meals with singing girls."

The monk winked at Xuân. "No problem! If you are willing to help promote the *Wooden Fish Drum*, to promote Buddhism, I mean, then I . . . I tell you frankly—I am here for little Master Blessing, the son of Buddha from the Perfume Pagoda . . ."

"What can you do for him, Sir?"

"I am a poor monk only. My role is to tend to his soul . . . Amitabha!"

"And I am educating the boy's body and his mother's, too!" Xuân said in a loud and dignified voice.

The monk scratched his ears casually and peered intently at Xuân. "Pardon me, Sir," he said. "Would you mind telling me your name, rank, and profession?"

"I am *Me sừ*[1] Xuân," he said, adopting a tone of superiority. "I was a student at the medical college and am now a tennis professor and the director of the Europeanization Tailor Shop for modern women!"

"You must be very well connected, no?"

"That goes without saying!"

"Sir, I entreat you to assist this poor monk . . . If you can help us to expand our base of support, we are prepared to offer you a 30 percent cut. Our business practices are completely legitimate, unlike those of our unscrupulous competitors at that new Buddhist Association. If you help to promote our newspaper, to increase our pagoda's base of support—"

"I can see that your idea of a religious life has several major shortcomings that need to be reformed," Xuân interrupted. "If you do not reform, you will not be completely up-to-date, and, if you are not completely up-to-date, you will be eliminated. During this ultra-modern era, even the Buddha will perish if he does not evolve along the path of civilization."

"That is true, sir! I can tell that you are a man of great learning and experience. This poor monk could certainly use your help . . . For example, if you were to advocate discretely on my behalf with Mrs. Senior Clerk and little Master Blessing, my standing and authority in their eyes will certainly be enhanced!"

"Yes, of course! But your group is not very skillful when it comes to the bottom line! Just take a look at the new Buddhist Association! They typically send a half-dozen monks and novices as fee-collecting ritual specialists to every funeral. That's good business. If I agree to help you, you must be willing to reform your old-fashioned ways!"

"The future of Buddhism lies in your hands, Sir! Amitabha!"

"In that case I insist on a 50 percent cut for my efforts."

"Please do not overcharge the Buddha. It is a grave sin."

Red-Haired Xuân slammed his fist down on the table. "In that case I will put up my own money and use the *Wooden Fish Drum* as a front only. I will take care of everything and let you have 20 percent."

---

1. *Monsieur.*

The monk rubbed his hands together. "Oh, please do not be so stingy with our pagoda. It is a grave sin."

They were still bargaining when Mrs. Deputy Customs Officer entered the room. She had changed into a traditional robe in order to meet the monk. "Amitabha! Greetings Venerable Teacher! Say hello little Master Blessing, show him how well behaved you are."

Red-Haired Xuân sat silently as the fashionable monk waxed eloquent, devising various expensive ceremonies and providing advice to Mrs. Deputy Customs Officer about the kinds of offerings she ought to make.

Chapter 14

The Way of the World

*

A Faithful Female Friend

*

Damn, Doctor Xuân Gets Angry

Over the next several days intense discussions about Red-Haired
Xuân took place at the Europeanization Tailor Shop and the house of
Grandpa Hồng. Two rival cliques emerged, one that supported Xuân
and one that opposed him. The opposition, led by Mr. ILL, included
High School Graduate Tân and the wife of the horned senior clerk.
Among Xuân's supporters were the horned senior clerk, Miss Snow,
the wife of Mr. ILL, several of the seamstresses, and virtually all of
the tailors. Hence, the majority remained in Xuân's camp. Grandpa
Hồng, Grandma, and the Civilizations refused to take a public stand
either way, preferring instead to wait and see which clique was
ascendent—a prudent strategy given the murkiness of the situation.

Members of Mr. ILL's opposition party were pleased now that
Xuân spent all of his time at the house of Mrs. Deputy Customs
Officer. To them this meant that he was no longer around to soil the
reputation of the Europeanization Tailor Shop. Xuân's supporters,
on the other hand, worried that his absence from the shop would be
bad for business.

Rumors circulated among both groups about an impending marriage between Xuân and Miss Snow. There were suspicions that
Grandpa Hồng had planted the rumors (a practice common with
government officials) in order to gauge public opinion before coming

134

out in support of or opposition to the union. If such were the case, the gambit failed because popular sentiment on the issue remained starkly divided. While some sneered at Xuân's origins in the lower classes, others praised him as a member of the common people. Given the subtlety of the distinction between these two groups (the lower classes and the common people), the debate raged on for days.

"Victor Ban said that Red-Haired Xuân used to be a vagabond," his detractors would say.

"Dr. Straight Talk respects Mr. Xuân very much," countered his supporters. "I've heard that they are close friends!"

"I know . . . What a pain! Shut up, already!" mumbled Grandpa.

"Let's not jump to conclusions," Grandma cautioned. "We should first find out if our girl has really misbehaved."

"Mr. Xuân is only a boyfriend," Miss Snow insisted, adopting the detached tone of a liberated woman.

For Mr. Civilization, Miss Snow's vague comments failed to convey a clear picture of the relationship between Xuân and his sister. Moreover, he had long espoused the view that unfettered social relations between men and women were a healthy sign of progress and Europeanization. Were Mr. Civilization to raise an objection to his sister's tryst, it might tarnish his progressive reputation. Hence, although he did not support his sister, he dared not criticize her behavior openly.

"Oh, to sow the seeds of civilization!" he complained self-righteously to himself. "What a heavy burden!"

In the meantime Xuân was juggling several jobs simultaneously: tennis professor, mentor to Master Blessing, and special advisor to Brother Tăng Phú concerning the reform and renovation of Buddhism. In his free time he made brief visits to the Europeanization Tailor Shop, where he liked to show off his erudition by critiquing and commenting on the latest fashions in the presence of the customers and staff. Mr. ILL's eyes reddened with rage as Xuân pointed out flaws in his designs, scolded his workers, or flirted shamelessly with his more fashionable female customers.

Sometimes he would stop by to ask a question. "Has Dr. Straight Talk arrived yet?" On other occasions he might utter a single statement. "Joseph Thiết needs a favor done; he told me to meet him here!"

Toward Miss Snow he was cold and formal. This hurt her but made others think that they were in love and planning to get married.

The more people discussed the matter at hand the less they agreed, and the more they argued the further they moved from the truth. Such is the way of the world. In the end each side began to doubt the veracity of its own arguments while growing simultaneously to hate the opposing side even more intensely.

Among his proponents there was one person who was especially grateful and committed to Xuân because of the support he had provided to her in the past. That was Mrs. ILL.

One afternoon, after sharing a huge meal of dog meat with a handful of devout monks, Xuân left the offices of the *Wooden Fish Drum* and headed for home. Red-faced and reeking of liquor, he happened unexpectedly upon the wife of Mr. ILL, who was out walking alone in one of her traditional outfits. To Xuân she looked miserable—the unlucky wife of a man dedicated to the progressive reform of society, on the one hand, and the cruel preservation of tradition within his own family, on the other.

"What have we here!" slurred Xuân drunkenly. "My *a mi*![1] Where are you off to all by your lonesome?"

Mrs. ILL was pleased that Xuân had addressed her in this daringly intimate and popular fashion. It had never happened to her before! She cautiously peered around to make sure that the street was deserted. Seeing that it was, she bravely and fashionably extended her hand to Red-Haired Xuân.

"What luck!" she said breathlessly. "I was just going to look for you, and here you are! I never see you at the Europeanization Tailor Shop anymore."

"I have been terribly busy lately," Xuân replied with an air of frivolous arrogance. "So much of my time these days is devoted to the development of the world of sports in general and tennis lessons in particular. I am also helping that utterly useless Dr. Straight Talk to educate the son of Mrs. Deputy Customs Officer. In addition, the head monk at the Lady Banh Pagoda has enlisted my help with his newspaper, the *Wooden Fish Drum.* How can I refuse? I do not want people to think that I am distant and unavailable! Therefore, I have had to leave to Mr. ILL the important responsibility of reforming

1. *Amie* (girlfriend).

society through custom-made clothes. I am sure you understand, my friend?"

"Yes, my friend," replied Mrs. ILL, bravely addressing Xuân with the same intimate pronoun. "I understand completely."

They began to walk together, side by side like boyfriend and girlfriend.

"But is that the only reason that you, my friend, have stopped coming by the Tailor Shop?" Mrs. ILL asked. "I trust we can be honest with each other. Please do not be offended if I ask you a question, my friend. Is it because of Miss Snow?"

"Idle gossip! Nonsense!" Xuân replied. "Miss Snow and I have nothing but a platonic relationship . . . just like the two of us!"

"So, why does everybody say otherwise?"

"What do they say?"

"They say that Grandpa Hồng wants you, my friend, to marry Miss Snow!"

Never before had Red-Haired Xuân heard such news, and it made him extremely happy. Still, he tried to maintain an air of dispassion. "That would be very dangerous if it were true! Of course, I would have to find a way to politely decline such an offer!"

Xuân's statement shocked Mrs. ILL. "But how could you possibly decline, my friend?" she retorted. "A woman like Miss Snow? Beautiful, very modern, and from a rich family? Were you to marry Miss Snow, every well-educated young man in our country of Nam would praise your prospecting skills! Not to mention that you two make such a perfect couple!"

Mrs. ILL's comments pleased Xuân immensely. Suddenly, however, he recalled Snow's conception of partial purity, as she had explained and demonstrated to him at the Fairyland Hotel. Although he knew that Miss Snow would never give up her virginity entirely before getting married, the idea of semi–virginity troubled him. He sighed to himself. "So many loves! Alas!"

"It must be so hard for you to decide, my friend!" Mrs. ILL replied. "Of course, you must choose carefully . . . "

"What scares me most is the prospect of sprouting horns. If I were to marry Miss Snow, my horns might grow so large that they could be ground into a powder and sold as traditional medicine."

Mrs. ILL smiled to herself. She recognized at that moment that all men are irrationally jealous—jealous of wind and shadows. Then she recalled how Xuân had supported her when she had endeavored to dress in a modern way. She felt overcome with a sense of gratitude.

"It seems that marriage—the so-called hundred-year knot—is not yet a high priority for you, my friend. I wonder why so many people are slandering and speaking ill of you in this regard . . . ?"

"Who? Whom do you mean?"

"I cannot name names. It will only breed more hatred and make me into a tattletale. The important thing is for you to be aware that such people are out there."

Ten more times Red-Haired Xuân asked for names but she refused to answer. Mrs. ILL was very proper indeed and hated the idea that she might be thought of as a tattletale.

"My only duty is to let you know that you are being maligned and slandered. It is said that you are from a lower-class family, that you are uneducated, and that you once worked as a ball boy and as an advertiser for venereal disease treatments. And that's not even the worst of it."

Red-Haired Xuân paused for a moment. "How terrible!" he said with a smirk. "If they dare to bad-mouth me like that, who knows what they will say about other people? The nature of my background and education are known to Mr. Civilization, Mrs. Deputy Customs Officer, the senior clerk, Dr. Straight Talk, and you, my dear friend. No doubt, those scurrilous rumors were spread by that bastard Victor Ban! At least Miss Snow knows what sort of person I am."

"How did you know it was Victor Ban?" Mrs. ILL asked immediately. "Indeed, it was he who told the story to Miss Snow's fiancé and who later confirmed it in a letter to Grandpa Hồng! The old man is humiliated."

"Do you know why Victor Ban hates me? I once helped him to open a drugstore back when I was in medical school. But I quit after discovering that he was adding bits of clay to the venereal disease medicine. Of course, he holds a grudge against me. I am not afraid of his hateful lies . . ."

Once she had been reassured about Xuân's lofty educational and social status, Mrs. ILL surmised that the time was right to tell Xuân of an important matter concerning his honor. "My dear friend," she began. "I have something important to tell you, but you must promise to keep it secret. Grandma Hồng has ordered that any of her relations who happen to meet you must immediately slap you or spit in your face."

Xuân was shocked. "Spit in my face? Slap me? Me? Did I not save the life of the most important old man in that family? Am I not the main reason that the Europeanization Tailor Shop has prospered as of late? That is how they choose to repay me? What a life . . . What a . . . Please excuse me . . . what a God-damned life!"

"Oh no! Please no!" responded Mrs. ILL. "Do not be so hot-tempered!"

"I will go directly over to her house," said Xuân haughtily, "so that she can spit in my face without delay!"

"No! I beg you!" she pleaded fearfully. "Please do not let them know that it was I who told you!"

But Xuân was inconsolable. As a reckless and truly uneducated man, he was unable to bear such a direct affront to his dignity. At that point even a harmless joke could have provoked him to murder. As Xuân's manner hardened, Mrs. ILL grew more and more frightened. He spun around and motioned to two rickshaw men. "Rickshaw! Rickshaw! Hey, you two! Come quick!"

Mrs. ILL pleaded with Xuân, but he ignored her. The rickshaw pulled up in front of them.

"Come along if you like," he said to her. "You'll see. I won't tell anyone that it was you, my friend, who told me. Don't worry. Maybe she won't really spit in my face."

Trembling with fear, Mrs. ILL got into the rickshaw. Thirty minutes later they pulled up in front of Grandpa Hồng's house. The two passengers paid their drivers and entered the front door.

Everyone in Grandpa Hồng's family was home. Great-Grandpa was slurping down a bowl of swallow's nest porridge. Grandpa Hồng was smoking a pipe of opium, assisted by the opium servant. Grandma, the Civilizations, Miss Snow, and High School Graduate Tân were sitting together in the living room. Xuân greeted everybody, but his face was dark with anger. He approached the bed of Great-Grandpa. "How are you, old man?" he said loudly. "Have you been sick since I cured you? Have you needed another doctor?"

The old man stopped eating. "Thank you very much, Doctor," he said. "I have felt fine ever since you cured me. I can't thank you enough, Doctor!"

"That's fine. No need to thank me!"

139

Xuân walked into the outer room and approached Mr. Civilization. "Since I stopped coming over to help, is your shop still
crowded with customers?"

"Yes! yes!" replied Mrs. Civilization on her husband's behalf.
"And many women and young ladies often ask about you."

"What do they ask about me for?" said Xuân with mock surprise.
"I'm a nobody! A low-class vagabond! A lowly ball boy! Not even
worth spitting on!"

Grandma kept her eyes down. "My goodness!" she exclaimed,
looking up gingerly. "Who would dare talk like that! Why say such a
thing, Doctor? Why do you seem so unhappy? Has anyone in this
family wronged you in any way?"

Miss Snow was pleased that her mother had adopted such a con-
ciliatory attitude. She whispered to Mr. ILL that it must have been
her ex-fiancé and Victor Ban who had slandered Xuân.

Xuân paced angrily back and forth. "I'm waiting for someone to
spit at me or to slap me in the face!"

Mr. and Mrs. Civilization were furious. They longed to unmask
Xuân there and then but were afraid of damaging their younger
sister's reputation in front of the wife of Mr. ILL and the opium
servant. Instead, they stood there fuming. Grandma was puzzled by
all the conflicting developments: Xuân's anger, the fact that he had
saved Great-Grandpa's life, the fact that her daughter, Miss Snow,
was now in love with him, the letter from Snow's fiancé. All of these
things confused her; she no longer knew right from wrong, good
from bad. "Please take a seat, Doctor," she said gently. "Who in this
family has said something against you?"

Xuân continued to pace back and forth. "If I get angry, it will
mean trouble for everyone! If I am wronged, everybody will suffer!"

No one dared to utter a peep, and the room fell silent. Xuân
paced back and forth across the floor for ten minutes. Only the
tapping of his shoes broke the silence. Just as his anger was beginning to dissipate, the horned senior clerk and his wife entered the
room, hand in hand. Xuân's mind jumped to the five piasters that
he owed Brother Tăng Phú for one "vegetarian meal" . . . "Sir," he
announced loudly, "you are a horned husband!"

Everyone was startled as if zapped by an electric shock. The senior postal clerk grabbed his chest and fell to the floor, moaning.

"Oh my parents! What shame! Now everyone knows of my wife's affair! The whole world knows! How shameful! How painful!"

Before Red-Haired Xuân realized the devastating effect of his words, a loud, distressing hiccup erupted from under the mosquito net of the old man's bed.

The family scurried in all directions. They divided into two groups: one lifted up the old man, and the other lifted up the senior clerk.

"Please! Oh Great Mandarin," Grandma implored Xuân. "Please, help cure my old man."

The old man moaned as if he were going to die. "No need for a cure! Just let me die! It is too shameful to live! If you want to cure something, then please cure the reputation of my family that you have sullied so!"

He hiccuped again. Tears welled up in Grandma's eyes. She begged Xuân to help . . . The whole house turned to Xuân . . . In the face of such a tragedy Xuân let down his guard. "It's true, Grandma," he murmured in a soft and honest voice. "I am completely uneducated. I was once a ball boy from a lower-class family. I know nothing about medicine!"

Fast as a thief, Xuân exited the house and ran away.

Grandma was regretful, but others criticized Xuân for allowing his hatred of the family to interfere with his professional duty. He did not really deserve to be a doctor, they thought.

Chapter 15

The Happiness of a Family in Mourning
☞
The Contribution of Civilization
☞
An Exemplary Funeral

Three days later the old man died.

In keeping with the theory that "too many cooks will spoil the soup," the family spent the days prior to his death bringing in all manner of quacks—Eastern quacks and Western quacks, old ones and young ones. Xuân remained out of sight during Great-Grandpa's demise, and, as a result, his medical reputation soared. Grandma sent people to find him but to no avail. Without Dr. Xuân all hope was lost; none of the real doctors could help the old man. When Dr. Straight Talk learned that his colleague Dr. Xuân was avoiding the patient, he also refused to take the case. Here was a lesson for those who dared to say that Xuân was from an uneducated, lower-class family, that he had been a vagabond and a ball boy . . . The herbalists Dr. Spleen and Dr. Lung were also asked to treat the patient, but, like the other respected doctors, they too refused. Another suggestion was to use the sacred medicine from the Bia Pagoda. In a recent case mud and buffalo shit taken from this source had been administered to patients suffering from tuberculosis and typhoid, and both had died. A subsequent investigation revealed that the sacred properties of the medicine had been falsely promoted by a band of village tyrants who had recently embezzled from the public budget. Hence, the medicine was no longer considered sacred. As a result of these various factors, the old man, already well into his eighties, died peacefully. During the chaos of his final days the opium servant calculated that Grandpa Hồng said "I know, what a pain. Shut up already!" exactly 1,872 times.

Great-Grandpa's death made many people happy. Grandpa Hồng told the horned senior clerk that he and his wife should expect to receive at least several thousand piasters. The senior clerk was pleasantly surprised that his invisible horns had proved so lucrative. He credited Xuân's advertising skills for netting such a valuable profit and planned to go into business with him in the future. If Xuân could generate several thousand piasters by saying "Sir, you are a horned husband!" imagine what he could make by saying "Sir, this product is the best. It should be sold overseas!" He planned to meet Xuân immediately so as to pay him the remaining five piasters that he owed him. One must demonstrate the value of one's word, he thought, before entering into business together.

Grandpa Hồng closed his eyes tightly and dreamed about how he would soon be able to wear funeral clothes, lean on a funeral cane, and cough, spit, and cry in public all at the same time. Everyone would look at him and say, "Oh, look how old the eldest son is!" Grandpa Hồng was very sure that the funeral and his funeral cane would leave a great impression.

The main concern of Grandpa's son, Mr. Civilization, was that a lawyer should witness the death of his paternal grandfather. This would ensure that the old man's will would actually be carried out in practice as opposed to existing solely in some theoretical netherworld. His only remaining worry was what to do with Red-Haired Xuân. While it was true that Xuân had committed two mistakes—he had seduced one of his younger sisters and denounced the lustful indiscretion of his other one—he had, inadvertently perhaps, provoked the propitious death of the old man. Two small mistakes, one big favor . . . how to react? Mr. Civilization rubbed his hands pensively through his hair. Fortunately, his puzzled visage resembled the face of someone mourning the death of a family member.

In fact, a sense of puzzlement and anxiety reigned over the whole affair. After the corpse was authenticated by the relevant authorities, the deceased party was wrapped in a shroud and left idle for over a day. Even though all the funeral plans had been long completed, Grandpa Hồng did not order the ceremony to begin. The younger generation—Grandpa's children and their spouses—began complaining about the slowness of the older generation. High School Graduate Tân was restless—eager to use the cameras that he had prepared for the occasion. Mrs. Civilization was anxious to wear her fashionable new mourning clothes. This outfit (including the white hat with black lace trim) had the potential to bring happiness to many grieving family members despite the painful death of a loved one. The delay of the funeral annoyed Mr. ILL because none of his new mourning designs appeared in public and hence were not covered in the press. Mr. Civilization was blamed for failing to intervene to end the delay. Grandpa Hồng was criticized for closing his eyes tightly and complaining about his "pain." Grandma was chided for following the old traditions too closely and generally stirring up trouble. The real reason for the delay was because of Miss Snow, or, more precisely, because of what Red-Haired Xuân had done to Miss Snow.

Grandma returned from Snow's fiancé's house. In front of the innocent eyes of the pious children and grandchildren waiting anxiously to bury the corpse of Great-Grandfather, she gestured silently for Mr. Civilization to follow her upstairs to Grandpa Hồng's room. Grandpa had just finished his sixtieth opium pipe of the day. The opium servant had stepped out for a moment, leaving the old man to enjoy the residue of opium left in his lungs. Upon seeing Grandma, he sat up. "What's going on, Grandma? Have they abandoned the marriage?"

Grandma sat down quietly next to him. Mr. Civilization also took a chair and sat down near the bed. "It's a dilemma," Grandma sighed. "They have not given up the marriage. They haven't done anything. The family is still coming here to express their condolences. How strange!"

"Why don't you tell them to move the wedding up before the funeral?"

"They do not want to move up the wedding. What can I do?"

"Are they going to do it or not? Do they still plan to marry their son to Snow, or do they think that she has been ruined? They must have some opinion?"

"What do you think they are thinking?" Grandma asked Grandpa.

"You're the one who went to their house," Grandpa snapped. "How come you're asking those of us who stayed home?"

Grandpa and Grandma continued to quarrel in a way common among old, traditional couples from respectable families—families in which husbands and wives never calmly discuss anything for more than fifteen minutes.

"In my opinion, I don't think that they are convinced that Snow has been ruined."

"No way! I think that they have always wanted to break up the marriage. Don't side with your child!"

"Why do you think they still want to express their condolences? Don't be stupid!"

"Perhaps it is some sort of trick! They do not cancel the marriage now, but they do not plan to go through with it either. That way no one else will dare to ask Snow's hand in marriage. She will die an old maid!"

"I'm not so sure! Maybe they are just as confused as we are. Even we do not know for sure whether our daughter has been ruined or not! When I told them that we should move the wedding date up before the funeral to save money rather than wait for three more years, they replied that their son is still young and only a student. They see no need to rush the wedding. They said that they could wait three or even five more years."

"So, what should we do now? I think we should ask Dr. Xuân to marry her before the funeral. If he agrees, then everything will be settled down."

Grandma bit her lip. She still remembered that Xuân had said, "If I am wronged, everybody will suffer!" He had also called attention to the horns of her son-in-law, the senior clerk, directly to his face, an announcement that brought shame to her other daughter. Xuân's hot temper was scary. She felt that she would be overcome with shame in his presence. It would be an honor to have such a noble son-in-law but also very frightening.

"There is an old saying," Grandma said, gesturing to her son, "'Children are spoiled by their mothers; grandchildren are spoiled by their grandmothers.' You have contributed to the ruin of Snow. You have made us all look bad. Now I ask for your advice."

"Yes!" Grandpa nodded. "What do you think, *toa*? A grown-up daughter at home is as dangerous as a bomb in the house. *Toa* should think of a way to send the girl off somewhere. That will put an end to our worries."

145

Mr. Civilization scratched his head and thought for a while. "I don't know. People already think that she loves Xuân. If we marry her off to Xuân before the funeral, aren't we admitting that she has been ruined by him? I say we ignore the whole mess and take care of the funeral first. Then, later on, if they still want their son to marry Snow, we'll do it. Otherwise, we'll marry her to Xuân. What's the rush?"

"Is it that easy?" Grandma asked. "Why did you say the other day that you're not sure if Xuân will agree?"

"If I persuade him, he will agree," Mr. Civilization responded.

Grandpa Hồng liked the idea of having a son-in-law like Xuân. Although he would have preferred everything settled then and there, he voiced agreement with his son's plan. Mr. Civilization furrowed his brow, trying to think of a way to wash away some of the nastier blemishes from Red-Haired Xuân's past. It was the only way to save face. While he had once been angry that so many people misunderstood Xuân in the past, this fact was now a source of solace. As with many fashionable men who made mistakes, he preferred to patch up what could be fixed rather than going through the embarrassment of admitting an error.

"Please do not worry, Mother and Father," he said, rising to his feet. "I will arrange an honorable marriage for Snow. Now, we should hold the funeral before it's too late."

The three descended the stairs and started to make arrangements for the funeral. The children and grandchildren were happy and pleased . . . Merrily, they went off to deliver the obituary, to order the clarinetists, and to rent the funeral cart. Many guests arrived to pay their respects, to make ritual offerings, and to express condolences.

The funeral began at exactly seven the next morning. Two policemen from the eighteenth precinct, Min toa and Min đơ, were hired to maintain order. They were pleased to get the work, since there had been few people to fine as of late, and they had begun to resemble businessmen on the verge of bankruptcy. Everyone in the family of the deceased seemed content, with the exception of Miss Snow. Why hadn't Xuân made ritual offerings? Why hadn't he attended the funeral? Had he lost respect for her? These questions nagged at Miss Snow; they made her so miserable that she thought of suicide. A needle pierced her heart as she looked in vain for her boyfriend among the crowd of mourners.

On the day of the funeral Miss Snow wore the outfit Innocence—a long, see-through dress over a bra with black lace trim that revealed her underarms and the top half of her breasts. She also wore a pretty mourning hat. With so many rumors swirling around about the defilement of her honor, Miss Snow selected Innocence to provide some reassurance that she had not lost her virginity completely. Carrying a small tray, she wandered among the crowd offering betel nuts and cigarettes. Her face looked vaguely sad and romantic, a fashionable mourning pose for the time. Close friends of Grandpa Hồng crowded around the coffin. Their jaws were covered with beards—long ones, short ones, black, red, and brown ones, some sparse, some dense, and some curly. Their faces were all set off by large pairs of ears. On their chests were dozens of medals: the Legion of Honor, the Imperial Medal, the Cambodian Medal, and the Ten Thousand Elephants Medal. They were moved by the mournful tones emanating from the clarinets and by the glimpses of Miss Snow's white arms and breasts that they managed to catch through her see-through dress.

Given the mixture of Vietnamese, Chinese, and French traditions on display, the funeral resembled a large festival. There was a large house made from paper and bamboo, a roasted pig under an umbrella, and a trumpet. There were scores of wreaths and at least three hundred banners displaying parallel couplets. Led by High School Graduate Tân, a handful of amateur photographers took pictures. There were hundreds of people there. Such a big funeral could almost bring a smile to the lips of the corpse in the coffin!

During the funeral procession Mr. ILL, his wife, Mrs. Deputy Customs Officer, and Mr. Joseph Thiết criticized Xuân's failure to make an appearance. As they passed the fourth intersection, the procession came to an abrupt halt as if stalled at a traffic accident. From one of the cross-streets six carts, each carrying a large umbrella and a team of monks from the Lady Banh Pagoda, merged into the procession right behind the flag carriers. Two huge mourning wreaths, one from the *Wooden Fish Drum* and one from Xuân himself were added to the procession. High School Graduate Tân hurriedly snapped several pictures before running back to inform his mother. Grandma ran forward, very moved by the fact that the wreaths were from Xuân, the famous doctor and advisor to the *Wooden Fish Drum*. It greatly enhanced the solemnity of the funeral.

"Thank Goodness for Mr. Xuân," she exclaimed. Otherwise, our funeral would have been small and inadequate!"

Brother Tăng Phú sat contentedly upon one of the carts. He was certain that his presence there would be seen as a victory for the *Wooden Fish Drum* and as a defeat for the new Buddhist Association.

After making sure that all his arrangements had been carried out correctly, Red-Haired Xuân joined the funeral procession. Miss Snow gazed at him lovingly, her face radiating gratitude. As usual, he was the object of intense praise and bitter jealousy.

The funeral procession made a strong impression wherever it went. It seemed that the whole city took notice of its size and pomp. It was just as Grandpa Hồng had wished. Mr. ILL and Mrs. Civilization were especially pleased with the public attention showered on the funeral fashions of the Europeanization Tailor Shop. Grandma was relieved that, far from being angry, Dr. Xuân had helped to make the funeral among the biggest and most honored in recent memory.

The funeral continued . . .

Vietnamese, Chinese, and French clarinets played on in turn. The mourners maintained somber expressions, all the while whispering excitedly to each other about their wives and their children, about the new houses and furniture they had purchased, or about the new clothes that they had had made. A large number of the mourners were young, fashionable lady friends of Miss Snow, Mrs. Civilization, Mrs. Sunset, and Mrs. Deputy Customs Officer. There were all sorts of fashionable men and women—flirting, courting, gossiping, teasing, arranging trysts, and making each other jealous—all the while maintaining the appropriately sorrowful expressions of mourners at a funeral. Interspersed with the requisite sobs and barbs that ring out at any funeral, the following whispered sentences were also overheard. "To whose family does that pretty girl belong? The one next to her is even hotter! Yes, yes, that bastard is a real creep!—Didn't his wife leave him?—Two husbands already!—She's not too old!—Those breasts look awfully French!—Can't you fix me up with her?—Did you say a gold mine or lead mine?—No more dates at all?—The wife is so fat, and the husband is so skinny. I see horns for him in the future!"

The funeral continued . . .

When the coffin was lowered into the tomb, High School Graduate Tân, in his long white mourning gown, forced each person to lean this way or that, to bend backwards or forwards, and to strike certain poses so that he could capture their presence at the moment the coffin was lowered into the ground. His friends jumped up and down on the surrounding tombs to get shots from different angles.

Holding his hat in his hand, Red-Haired Xuân stood solemnly next to the horned senior clerk. When Grandpa Hồng coughed and spit and cried and fell unconscious to the ground, the horned senior clerk began to wail: "Wa! . . . Wa! . . . Wa!"

Everybody remarked on the good behavior of the nephew-in-law.

The horned senior clerk cried so much that he almost fainted, and Xuân had to help him up. But, despite his best efforts, Xuân could not hold him straight. In his huge white turban and long white mourning gown, the senior clerk continued to wail. "Wa! . . . Wa! . . . Wa! . . ."

Red-Haired Xuân wanted to release him. Suddenly, he felt the senior clerk slipping a folded-up five piaster note into his hand. He held it so that no one could see it. Then he went to look for Brother Tăng Phú, who was lost among the three hundred mourners.

Chapter 16

A Glorious and Happy Misunderstanding!
●
Red-Haired Xuân Conquers the Police

Mr. Civilization caught a glimpse of Xuân. "The bastard looks less like a vagabond everyday," he thought to himself. "Clothes and food really make a difference. Now, how to approach this? How to make him register his name at the General Department without causing a fuss? How to explain that, since I plan to marry my sister to him, I need to elevate him from a lowly ball boy to a tennis amateur? Perhaps I should just be straight with him?"

As he was mulling all this over, Xuân opened the gate and extended a hand. "What's up? Madame Senior Clerk has taken little Master Blessing to the Lady Banh Pagoda to request a written good luck prayer."

"Are you busy?"

"I'm free as a bird. By the way, your wife's game is getting better every day."

Mr. Civilization ignored the compliment. "You should go upstairs and change into some decent clothes," he said abruptly. "We've got somewhere to go and important work to do!"

"What is it?"

"Don't ask. Just go change your clothes."

Civilization waited ten minutes before Xuân returned, properly

150

attired. Xuân's old boss called two rickshaws but did not reveal their destination to him. Xuân had no idea where they were going.

"Hey, what about the rumor that you ruined my sister? We're going to clean up this sordid mess right now!"

Red-Haired Xuân was scared. He imagined that they were off to the Police Station, the Department of Counter-Espionage, or the Court, where he would be locked up and subjected to unspeakable tortures as punishment for ruining a respectable girl from a good family. He paused for a moment before the rickshaw.

"Maybe the bastard won't marry my younger sister," Mr. Civilization thought to himself. "Or maybe they've done nothing together, and all the rumors are nonsense."

"I have made a horrible mistake, Monsieur," Xuân blurted out, interrupting Civilization's train of thought. "I want to apologize. Snow loves me, and I love Snow. If you try to keep us apart, it will kill us. We have been together already."

Mr. Civilization was shocked. There was no longer any doubt about it! His younger sister had been ruined! If Snow did not marry Xuân, then nobody would marry her! There was nothing to do now but to try to save as much face as possible.

"It's no matter," he said resolutely. "We can solve this. But first we have to make you more respectable. I want you to register your name at the General Athletic Department as an amateur tennis player. Then you will be able to compete for the championship against the top players in all of Tonkin. I want my younger sister to marry an athlete, not a ball boy."

"So, we're going to the General Athletic Department?"

"Yes! I am a progressive person. I do not distinguish between the different classes! As a devoted sports fan, I first recognized your potential athletic value to our country and decided to rescue you on the day you were fired. Isn't that right? Since you've been working for us, your social status has gradually improved. Today you are a different person. It is no accident that you fell in love with my sister! . . . It was probably predestined. In any case, I always intended for my sister to marry you. It is only because of my efforts that you have become what you are today!"

Xuân's image of the General Athletic Department contrasted agreeably with what he knew of the Police Station, the Department of Counter-Espionage, and the Court. Still, he recalled his inglorious past and felt himself unfit to be Snow's husband. He thought it best to refuse Civilization's offer. "Monsieur, Snow only loves me because you once jokingly told Great-Grandfather that I was a medical student. It will be a terrible mistake for Snow to marry me. I will be deceiving an honorable girl."

Xuân's words made Civilization ashamed. He had caused a huge injustice, all on account of a harmless white lie. "No matter!" he said, trying to assuage his own guilt. "You actually do know something about medicine. But, because diplomas mean everything in this old-fashioned society, I had to stretch the truth a little. It doesn't matter if you are a medical student or not, I still want you to marry my sister."

"You are too kind, Monsieur," Xuân replied sadly. "But I urge you to reconsider! Snow is beautiful, rich, and from a modern and cultivated family. As you know, I was orphaned during my childhood. I worked as a ball boy and sold roasted peanuts on the street. I did many lowly jobs. I do not deserve her."

Mr. Civilization frowned. "Tricky bastard!" Mr. Civilization thought to himself. "Why does he needle me like this? A dowry like my sister's, and still he holds out for more! I guess he's after some sort of guarantee, the greedy bastard!"

"It's no matter! There are no lowly jobs, only lowly people. Take me, for instance; I have the mind of a common person. And I would love nothing more than to have a common, younger brother-in-law like you. Moreover, Snow has her own fortune. You will not have to worry about hard work anymore if you agree to marry her. You can concentrate on promoting sports in our nation for the remainder of your life."

Xuân remained unconvinced. "No, I dare not accept. Please reconsider your offer."

"Monsieur," Mr. Civilization replied threateningly, his voice rising in anger, "this is a matter for your conscience! You have ruined the reputation of a girl from a respectable family. I want to solve this problem. It may bode ill for your future if you refuse to help me."

The threat scared Xuân. "Yes, yes," he replied meekly, "I will do whatever you think is best."

Mr. Civilization sighed. He was overcome with a sensation of happiness and relief, commonly felt among people who succeed in forcing others to marry against their will. Satisfied that the marriage would go forward, he motioned for Xuân to get in the rickshaw.

Arriving at the General Athletic Department, Red-Haired Xuân felt the road to fame and success opening wide before him. The driveway was full of beautiful cars. Elegantly clad Vietnamese and French men entered and exited along with fashionable Vietnamese ladies and French madames. They all exuded the luxurious air of the upper classes. Xuân knew that he had truly arrived. Oh, sports! Glorious sports! What can't you accomplish? Hip hip hooray!

As his mind raced with various lofty ideas about the future of our race, Mr. Civilization led him to a large, solemn-looking office. On the walls were paintings of tennis and boxing matches, fencing contests, swimming races, pole vaulting tournaments, bicycle competitions, racing cars, round footballs, and not-so-round footballs. Many people approached Mr. Civilization and Red-Haired Xuân to shake their hands. As conversations unfolded noisily in French, a look of scorn and annoyance passed over Xuân's face. His expression suggested a profound reverence for the mother tongue and resentment toward those who used French when it was unnecessary. The French speakers seemed equally annoyed with Xuân's attitude.

Mr. Civilization thought it best to introduce Xuân immediately. "Messieurs, this is my friend Xuân, a tennis professor. He is here to register on the list of tennis amateurs. He is a great hope for Tonkin."

One of the intellectuals turned to Xuân and addressed him at some length in French. Xuân pursed his lips in disgust. "Please, Sir," he retorted sternly, "isn't our language good enough for you?"

"Yes, of course, please forgive me!" the man replied sheepishly, acknowledging his disrespect to the mother tongue. "Sir, I have long heard your name and am pleased to have the honor of meeting you at last."

Xuân bowed his head. "I am honored!"

"Thank you very much, Sir! I have seen you play many times, and I admire you. You have a bright future. We have been worried that Tonkin has no one who can compete against Annam and Cochinchina, but now we are fortunate to have you. Our Majesty will be so pleased if you defeat the champions of Annam and Cochinchina and go on to represent Indochina in Siam."

"I long for nothing more."

They shook hands solemnly and said good-bye. As the director of the General Athletic Department had yet to arrive, everyone took the opportunity to make the acquaintance of everyone else. Hence, Xuân was able to meet a wide range of amateur tennis players, including several sons of province chiefs and governors. Everyone declared that they "hoped to have the honor" of playing against Xuân for the championship in the near future. He was inundated with praise and compliments. Those confident of defeating him displayed a false modesty, while those who were afraid they would lose to Xuân were careful not to offend him.

Sports reporters from three daily newspapers vied to interview him. The fact that a tennis professor—a tennis professional, in other words—had registered his name on the amateur list was big news in sporting circles. Civilization knew that he had to promote Xuân's reputation carefully, so he remained by his side like a faithful dog beside its master. He was afraid that he would lose face if Xuân made an embarrassing gaffe. But Xuân was cautious, well behaved, and maintained the scornful visage of a genuine member of the upper classes. When faced with a difficult question, Xuân simply smacked his lips, clicked his tongue, and gestured haughtily to Mr. Civilization. "Please, my manager will answer that question."

The arrangement was not without benefits for Civilization. Whenever journalists took Xuân's photo as "the hope of Tonkin," they allowed his manager to stand next to him in the picture.

Striking a pose often adopted by talented and confident men, Xuân would occasionally tap Civilization on the shoulder and whisper intimately into his ear: "You will ride my coattails to fame and success just like the managers of Chim and Giao before you! Thanks to me, you will also become a household name."

Mr. Civilization realized that what Xuân said was probably true, even though it was he who was masterminding Xuân's reputation.

After signing his name in the register in front of a handful of French men and the chairman of the Athletic Council, Xuân and his manager completed a final round of handshakes and sauntered out of the office. Turning a corner, they ran smack into two policemen. It was like a head-on collision between automobiles. Immediately, Xuân recognized the two officers as Min đơ and Min toa from the Eighteenth Precinct. One of the officers opened his notebook and took out a pencil to write a ticket. "We entered on the right side. But you two Monsieurs entered on the left. Names please?!"

"That's crazy!" Civilization protested. "There is no such law. We are inside a building, not out on the street. You can't fine us in here!"

"Nice try, but you Messieurs are guilty of hitting officers of the state and of preventing us from carrying out our work . . ."

Red-Haired Xuân thrust his chest forward. "I am *Me sừ* Xuân, tennis professor. I am the great hope of Tonkin!"

The policemen looked hesitantly at each other. After a moment one thrust his own chest forward. "I am *Me sừ Min đơ*, an officer of the fourth rank and owner of a victory medal. I won first prize in the Tour de Hanoi–Hà Đông and second prize in the Tour de Hanoi–Đồ Sơn. I represent the future of the police."

The other officer followed his friend's example. "I am *Me sừ Min toa*, an officer of the fifth rank and winner of the first prize in the Hanoi–Nam Định Cup, the Laundry Boy Cup, and the Melia Jaune Cup. I represent the glory of the Hanoi Police and a great hope of Indochina!"

Transfixed by their own credentials, the officers stood there in silence, forgetting to write the tickets.

"I guess good policemen need this sort of background," Mr. Civilization said encouragingly.

"We need no other training," one of the officers said in agreement. "We have sixteen streets to patrol day and night. Our training regimen is even more rigorous than that of Bổng and Cổng!"[1]

"And our bicycles are completely normal," the other officer added. "We practice *ru-líp*[2] in crowded streets! It prepares us for long-distance races. Since we rarely write tickets, bicycle training helps us to overcome our boredom! Long live sports! Long live the police!"

"It seems that we all are comrades!" said Red-Haired Xuân, nodding his head.

"Quite right! Quite right!" the officers responded in unison. "But we can still write you a ticket!"

"We are all working for the future of sports and the glorification of our race!" Xuân said.

---

1. Well-known racing cyclists.
2. *Roue libre* (freestyle).

"That goes without saying, but it is irrelevant!"

"On the contrary. Our recent collision was little more than a sporting accident. How can you write a ticket for a sporting accident?"

The officers hesitated. They looked at each other, trying to determine whether Xuân's comment was strictly legal.

"Forget about it," Xuân continued. "Soon we will be sitting together at the emperor's banquet for sports champions. How can you even consider writing us a ticket? It's heartless!"

"This whole thing is absurd," yelled Mr. Civilization. "It's illegal to write such a ticket. We have broken no law!"

Officer Min toa waved his hand.

"We're policemen, for goodness sake! Our concern is tickets, not laws! Only ordinary people worry about transgressions of the law, not officers of the state! If you say that we are violating the law, you are interfering with the duty of state officers!"

"You make perfect sense," said Red-Haired Xuân. "But enough already! You must be here to register your names?"

"Yes, for the Ha Noi—Tourane *Sa Majesté* Cup!"

"Then we are all in this sporting village together. We are all glorifying our race. If you write us a ticket, we will become enemies. It is better to be friends. We should help each other! We should promote each other!"

"How do you mean?"

"You will spread the word that I am a talented tennis player, the great hope of Indochina . . ."

"And what about us?" the officers asked.

"We will tell everyone that you are the best cycling officers around; that you always carry out your duties diligently, maintain law and order in the city, and that you will certainly win the Tour de Hanoi—Saigon. And we will insist that you deserve promotions . . . How does that sound?"

The officers nodded, shook hands with Civilization and Xuân, and put away their tickets. They had fulfilled their duties as policemen and followed the law to the letter.

Chapter 17

The Fiancé
◓

A Rape Case
◓

An Official Investigation

My darling!" exclaimed Miss Snow. "I am so happy! Who could have imagined that our marriage plans would succeed so easily? I'm so happy I could just die! I want to commit suicide!"

Oblivious to the romantic and poetic dimensions of her statement, Xuân frowned deeply. "Suicide! We are about to get married, and you want to commit suicide?!"

Miss Snow pointed to the White Bamboo Lake. "If we were to jump to our deaths together into those silvery waves, the country would talk forever about our passionate love affair. But never mind—I'm only joking. Your frightened expression pleases me; it means that you truly love me."

"How difficult you are, my dear," Xuân snapped in reply. "Who could indulge you more than I!"

They set off on a leisurely walk. It was eight in the morning, but the sun had yet to appear through the dense layers of white clouds. Perhaps it did not want to disturb the young lovers. The wind blew gently. Xuân and Miss Snow had planned a classic tryst: a lengthy walk along Old Fish Road. Xuân related the whole story about how Mr. Civilization had insisted that he marry Miss Snow. Although this hurt her self-esteem a little, she was still happy. Given that Xuân had actually been forced to marry her, Miss Snow's suicidal impulse was indeed appropriate. Both Xuân and Snow were very content.

"My darling Snow," Xuân said dreamily, "do you know why I fell in love with you?"

"Because I am so honest?"

"Because you are so silly. You relied on me to ruin your respectable reputation. Why did you place such trust in me?"

Miss Snow shrugged her shoulders. "Because I am honest! Remember when I allowed you to check whether I used rubber breasts?"

"That's right! Thanks to those rubber breasts, we came to appreciate each other's honesty! Our happiness is the result of those rubber breasts—the rubber breasts of social reform . . . "

Miss Snow shrieked with joy. "Long live Europeanization! Long live rubber breasts!"

Suddenly, Miss Snow spied something in the distance that made her frown. It was a young man running toward them wearing traditional clothes: a turban, a floor-length silk gown, and a pair of old-fashioned shoes. Miss Snow stamped her feet in annoyance.

"It's my old fiancé, the one I rejected to marry you. He probably wants to quarrel with me! I really don't want to see him. I'll let you handle this. Go ahead and teach him a lesson. I'll wait for you at Mrs. Deputy Customs Officer's house. We'll talk later."

Miss Snow turned and flagged a rickshaw. Xuân nodded good-bye to her. Then he folded his arms and waited for the quarrel to begin.

The young man approached Xuân and greeted him with his hands together, in the manner of a traditional Confucian scholar. Red-Haired Xuân dismissed the gesture. "How old-fashioned! Not evolved at all! Sports! Social reform!"

The young man was both frightened and angry. "Sir . . . ," he stammered, "Permit me to introduce myself . . . I am the fiancé of Miss Snow, the one who just ran away!"

Red-Haired Xuân bowed his head. "I am honored," he said, puffing out his chest. "I am *Me sừ* Xuân, tennis professor, the hope of Tonkin!"

The young man recognized that Xuân had seized the upper hand. "It is I who am honored! Forgive me for disturbing you, Sir. Even though you are talented, you should not try to harm other people. If I am not mistaken, you are in the process of stealing my wife. Please,

Sir. I am not famous. I have no talent. Where is the victory in defeating me?"

Red-Haired Xuân unleashed one of his now famous second-hand speeches on the young man. "You . . . are unfashionable and old-fashioned! You are unreasonable! I am a member of the Europeanization Movement. The future fate of our nation—whether it evolves toward civilization or descends into barbarity—lies in my hands! Never mind what those old-fashioned moralists say! We do not only 'reform the outside'! Our society will progress according to the basic laws of evolution. During this deeply reformist era, everything conservative will be eliminated! You are not Europeanized enough! You are an obstacle along the road of evolution! Sports . . . Race . . . Health! What is family happiness if not the happiness of husbands and their wives?"

"But . . . I am also from a decent family," the young man replied. "I have a diploma from a good secondary school. In terms of family background, I am the son of a senior clerk and the grandson of a district chief . . . I am more than a suitable match for Miss Snow. Why has she changed her attitude toward me so?"

"But are you from a common family?" Xuân replied tersely. "Do you have a popular background? How strange you are! You do not understand contemporary mores! Don't you know what is fashionable today?"

The young man seemed embarrassed! Not only were his clothes old-fashioned, but his background was unfashionably respectable! Everything about him was wrong.

Before he could muster a response, Xuân raised his hand and continued: "I am from a lower-class family! In the past I sold roasted peanuts on the street and Tiger Balm aboard the trains. I even worked as an errand boy for the theater! And still I am able to marry Grandpa Hồng's daughter! What do you think of that?"

Xuân's statement frightened the jilted fiancé. He guessed that Xuân was sarcastically repeating the baseless rumors spread about him by Victor Ban. In fact, he imagined, Xuân must come from an extremely exalted background. The young man squirmed painfully like a worm under a boot. "If you insist, Monsieur, I will concede. But, as a man of honor, I must warn you that we are now life-and-death rivals. Do not forget it!"

The young man bowed politely and left. His threat troubled Red-

Haired Xuân, who stood mulling it over for several minutes. He hailed a rickshaw and returned home, where his betrothed awaited him. A sense of contentment returned to Xuân after he reflected on the lesson that he had just taught the young man. The life-and-death rivalry was not worth worrying about, he surmised, because of the great difficulty involved in actually killing someone.

When he arrived home, it was 10:00 A.M. and Miss Snow was leafing through a photo album, waiting for him. Mrs. Deputy Customs Officer and little Master Blessing had yet to wake up. Xuân was happy for the respite, even if it was only for a half-hour. Now he could talk to his girlfriend without fear of being disturbed.

"Did you teach him a lesson, my darling?"

"Of course. I explained, with perfect logic, why he has no hope with you. I showed him that it is pure folly for him to compete with me! It turns out that he is not an unreasonable person. In the end he accepted our wedding plans and wished us a hundred years of happiness!"

"He wished us happiness?"

"Yes! He said: 'It is better that Snow marries you than me . . . Because I love Snow, I only want to see her happy.'"

Miss Snow jumped up and embraced Xuân around the neck. "You deserve a thousand kisses as a reward!"

Red-Haired Xuân stepped forward to receive his hard-earned and well-deserved kisses. "Now . . . " he whispered in her ear. "I . . . want to truly ruin your life!"

Miss Snow pursed her lips in a manner so moral she appeared truly beyond reproach. "Hey! Hey! Forget it! You know that I am still a romantic."

Miss Snow pushed Xuân aside. "Careful," she whispered, "or we'll be caught red-handed!"

Xuân shook his head. "Mrs. Deputy Customs Officer and her son are still sleeping."

"What about the servants?"

"They are in the back of the house! Quiet. Please permit me to love you. You should be more obedient . . ."

Fearing that she would be considered disobedient, Miss Snow relented, and they moved to the *đi văng*.[1] Miss Snow closed her eyes.

---

1. *Divan* (sofa).

Her expression suggested that she was dreaming about how the cancellation of her previous engagement and the recent revolution in her petty, old-fashioned family was about to bring her a great dose of individual happiness. At that moment she longed to write a novel about her life to provide an example for liberated women in the future.

Suddenly, the door swung open, and Mrs. Deputy Customs Officer rushed in, an angry expression on her face. The lovers were startled and released each other. When had she awakened? Mrs. Deputy Customs Officer was still in her sleeping gown. She poked her finger in Miss Snow's face like a jealous wife. "Is my house a brothel? Do you know that you are dirtying my house, Miss? Do you know that your behavior is loose and immoral? Get out of my house immediately! You bring shame upon me!"

Appropriately embarrassed, Miss Snow got up and left.

Mrs. Deputy Customs Officer turned to Xuân. "How can you be so thoughtless? Don't you know what a bad thing you've done? How dare you try to ruin the life of a decent girl like that?"

Xuân shrugged his shoulders. "What I was doing was for the benefit of that decent girl!"

"Benefit?"

"Yes! Snow is my fiancée! Yesterday Mr. Civilization insisted that I marry her! It is you who are damaging our honor!"

Mrs. Deputy Customs Officer was struck dumb like a wooden statue. Her sleeping gown, however, revealed as much as if she had actually been nude. The seductive image exerted a strange obsessive power over Xuân, who was already angry and excited. In search of release he grabbed the faithful widow and held her in a tight embrace.

Meekly attempting to maintain her fidelity toward her two ex-husbands, Mrs. Deputy Customs Officer uttered a few words of protest before being pulled down to the couch. "Hey, Mr. Xuân! Why are you acting so funny?"

But at that moment our Red-Haired Xuân did not care about propriety or morality. He was determined to get some release and so pretended to be deaf. Mrs. Deputy Customs Officer moaned but in a low voice, like a faithful widow.

"Oh my goodness! It's killing me! I'm being raped!"

Outside the door screams echoed out. "No way! No way!"

Little Master Blessing rushed downstairs. Mrs. Deputy Customs

Officer stopped moaning. "Don't worry. He's just looking for his nanny!"

She continued to moan but softly, so as not to be interrupted. "It's killing me! Oh my neighbors and my fellow villagers! I am so miserable! Please help me!"

Five minutes later there was a knock at the door. The two hurriedly arranged their clothes and moved to chairs in different corners of the room.

"Come in," Mrs. Deputy Customs Officer said in a loud, dignified voice.

In walked Officers Min đơ and Min toa. They were followed by little Master Blessing's nanny and the cook.

"Madame," said one of the officers, "we have been called to rescue you!"

"What? Who called policemen into this house? Why do I need to be rescued? Was it the nanny or the cook? Oh, you are both so insolent!"

The cook blanched.

"But Madame," he stammered, "when little Master Blessing called me upstairs, I heard someone moaning. I was frightened."

"We were out on the street when he called us in!" Min toa explained.

"Moaning? Oh yes! I was reading a detective story aloud for the teacher here to listen to," replied the quick-witted Mrs. Deputy Customs Officer.

Officer Min đơ laughed heartily. "That's funny! We thought someone was being raped!"

The mistress turned angrily to her servant. "If you make a mistake like that again, I will cut your god-damned throat! You stupid pig!"

"How god-damned insolent!" Xuân added.

Everyone stared uneasily at each other. To break the tension, Red-Haired Xuân introduced the two policemen to the still-dignified mistress.

"Allow me to introduce Officer Min đơ, a policeman of the fourth rank and recent winner of the Medal of Victory. He earned first prize in the Tour de Hanoi–Đồ Sơn and second prize at the Tour de Hanoi–Hà Đông. He represents the future of the police! . . . And here we have Officer Min toa: winner of the Laundry Boy Cup and the Melia Jaune Cup. He is the glory of the Hanoi Police and a great hope of Indochina!"

The officers then dutifully introduced Xuân to Mrs. Deputy Customs Officer. "This is Monsieur Xuân, a tennis professor and the hope of Tonkin!"

Xuân feared it would be impolite if no one introduced Mrs. Deputy Customs Officer. "Permit me to introduce Mrs. Senior Clerk, a woman who remains faithful to her two ex-husbands, a kind mother and great patron of the world of sports!"

Everyone was pleased. The two officers, however, were still a little disappointed that they had been unable to carry out their duties. "We were called to investigate a rape case!" explained one of the officers. "But it appears that nothing has transpired. It is not right to toy with officers of the state. We do not come here for nothing!"

"Madame," added the other officer, "you must understand the nature of our responsibilities. Although we would like to 'live and let live' . . . we have wasted valuable time and energy rushing over here. We need to write some kind of ticket. It is not acceptable to disturb officers of the state. If there is no rapist to punish, at least allow us to ticket you for letting your dog run in the street without a leash."

Eager to put the case behind her, Mrs. Deputy Customs Officer nodded her assent. "It's up to you."

It was an agreeable resolution for all involved. Mrs. Deputy Customs Officer retained her reputation for unswerving fidelity to her two ex-husbands. Red-Haired Xuân avoided a prison sentence. And the police station of the Eighteenth Precinct did not have to waste its time with a complicated investigation.

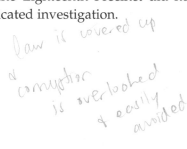

law is covered up & corruption is overlooked & easily avoided

Chapter 18

A Plot
⌖

Red-Haired Xuân Spies on the Police
⌖

A Doctor's Promise

Red-Haired Xuân stepped off the tennis court. There was only one more week before the emperor embarked on his imperial journey to the North, and, since Mrs. Civilization hoped to win the Women's Cup, Xuân had to practice with her constantly. It was almost seven o'clock and dark outside when they ended their session. Xuân turned down a dinner invitation from his manager (that's right—his manager!), Mr. Civilization. He had something important on his mind . . .

What a pain! That afternoon Mrs. Deputy Customs Officer had whined, in that poetic way of hers, that he should help salvage her reputation as a faithful widow. For some unknown reason their secret love affair—if we can call it that—had been completely exposed. It had become a source of rumors and near-constant gossip.

"My darling," Mrs. Deputy Customs Officer had said to Xuân in a heart-rending voice, "do you know what you have done to my honor?"

Ever considerate of other people, Xuân acknowledged that he had despoiled a virtuous woman. He was full of regret but could not undo what he had done, nor could he control the rampant spread of lurid stories. It was as if the walls had ears and the forest veins!

As he strolled the streets like a philosopher—hands in his pockets, racket tucked under his arm—Xuân spied the shriveled, weather-beaten old fortune-teller. He was walking with an umbrella on one shoulder and an old pair of shoes in his hand. He greeted Xuân but dared not ask too many questions. Recalling that he owed his fame and position partly to the fortune-teller, Red-Haired Xuân thought it would be a decent gesture to express his gratitude by treating the old man to a big meal. Although he had earned a few piasters by reading the fortune of Mrs. Deputy Customs Officer, the fortune-teller remained as poor as before.

"So, you are not making much money lately?"

"No, sir, not at all!"

"I would like to invite you to eat and drink with me. We have many things to talk about."

The fortune-teller agreed. Xuân called rickshaws, and a half-hour later the two sat at the counter in the Triều Châu Hotel on Hàng Buồm Street. The restaurant was very crowded. It seemed that all of Hanoi was feverishly preparing to welcome the king. The Protectorate Government planned to organize five days of festivals during which many new and unusual games would be played. Rumor had it that not only was our emperor planning to visit the North but that the king of a neighboring country might be there as well. And not merely the king of Cambodia or Laos but the king of Siam.[1] The reason for his visit was that Germany and Japan had recently persuaded the Siamese government to attempt to reclaim traditional lands from Indochina by publishing a map in which the territory of Siam extended beyond the Hoành mountain range. To maintain peace in the Far East the Indochinese government implemented a skillful diplomatic policy. Newspapers from all three regions denounced the Siamese as barbarians while simultaneously singing the praises of the Vietnamese—describing them as the children of dragons and the grandchildren of fairies whose culture and literature stretched back thousands of years. As a result, the papers continued, the Vietnamese were not afraid of the Siamese and would willingly fight them if necessary. To try to improve relations between the countries, on the one hand, and to let the arrogant Siamese

1. The novel takes place after the king of Siam, Prajadhipok, had abdicated in 1935 and was replaced by a ten-year-old king then living in Switzerland. The adult king who appears in the novel is identified, however, as Prajadhipok (p. 183). No explanation is provided for this anachronism.

know that we are the children of dragons and the grandchildren of fairies, on the other, the Protectorate Government invited the king of Siam to travel to Vietnam. Hence, all of Hanoi was busily making arrangements to welcome the two monarchs. The Triều Châu Restaurant was bursting with people who were to benefit from the festivities or were required to play a role in them—contractors, spies, businessmen, dancing girls, artists, and athletes.

After ordering a range of dishes and several rounds of alcohol, Red-Haired Xuân prepared to ask the fortune-teller (the modern-day reincarnation of Quỷ Cốc Tử and Gia Cát) about his future—his children, marriage, fame, and honor—and about his affair with Mrs. Deputy Customs Officer. Suddenly, he overheard his name mentioned in a conversation taking place on the other side of a wooden panel. He winked to the fortune-teller and gestured for him to listen in.

Two people were speaking.

"You said his name is Red-Haired Xuân? What does he look like?"

"I will take you to the tennis court tomorrow afternoon and show him to you. You must know his face so that we can act on the day the king arrives . . ."

They were silent for a moment. Xuân frowned and looked at the fortune-teller, who had started drinking well before the food arrived.

The voices continued. "We should teach him a lesson right away!"

"No! I want him in jail! He has made my life miserable. I am an educated man! I will not be satisfied with less than five years in jail and ten years in exile. I have a plan already. Just promise you will help me."

"I promise. But what's the plan? It must be a good one!"

"It's very good! Not only will my rival end up in jail, but he will miss the tennis tournament! Once we take action, we must go all the way. Otherwise, there's no point. I will print up leaflets saying, 'Down with the King of Siam!' When the king makes his entrance, I will sneak up behind Xuân, and you will stand next to him!"

"What then?"

"You will slip several of the leaflets into the pockets of his shirt and pants."

"What about you?"

"Me? My role is even more heroic than yours. I will scream: 'Long live the Popular Front Government! Long live Democratic France!'

Naturally, policemen and undercover security agents will arrest us immediately . . ."

"Oh no!"

"But then only those found to have leaflets in their pockets will be taken into custody. The two of us will bear witness to the fact that it was Xuân who yelled the slogan. We will be released immediately."

"I see! But why will they arrest someone for yelling: 'Long live the current government! Long live Democratic France!'?"

"That's easy! Although France, which rules over us, is a democracy, we are a monarchy with a king. Siam is also a monarchy! To welcome the kings with slogans supporting democracy implies a desire to overthrow the monarchy! The Protectorate Government is very sensitive about this sort of thing. If we scream, 'Long live Democratic France!' I guarantee that somebody will be arrested."

"What a clever plan! But please lower your voice."

"Yes, but you must scream loudly when the time comes."

"Of course! I will put my whole heart into it! Please, another bottle of liquor!"

Red-Haired Xuân stood up and peered through a small hole in the wooden panel. There he saw the ex-fiancé of Miss Snow eating and drinking with a man wearing shorts, Chinese shoes, a cap, and his hair up in a bun. The man resembled a certain kind of old-fashioned gangster. After committing the man's face to memory, Xuân calmly returned to his table and resumed drinking with the fortune-teller.

The waiter brought several dishes of delicious food, which the fortune-teller hungrily devoured.

"The stars this month suggest that some kind of ambush is in store for you."

"Meaning?"

"There is someone who hates you and wishes you harm. You must be very careful! But there are also indications that you will be protected by a special star sent from heaven!"

The fortune-teller punctuated his prophesy by gracefully dropping an entire roasted sparrow into his mouth. Before Xuân could pick up the conversation, he noticed two men at a nearby table who resembled secret police agents. Their pants were cuffed in a way distinctive of police officers, suggesting that they actually hoped to be recognized, despite their undercover status. Red-Haired Xuân moved his seat closer so as to eavesdrop on their conversation. He was spying on the spies.

"We have received our orders! The destiny of society lies in our hands. Our mission is top secret. You must not tell a soul!"

"I await your briefing, Sir."

"State policy is now unambiguous on this matter. Until the arrival of the king, your job is to spy on those who falsely advocate policies of Franco-Vietnamese harmony, Franco-Vietnamese friendship, and direct rule. You must be vigilant against anyone who says, 'Long live the Popular Front Government!' or 'Down with Fascism!' You must also be on the lookout for people who imitate the French in France by greeting each other with raised hands, as if they planned to hit one another!"

"Sir . . . Sir . . . Why are we suspicious of Franco-Vietnamese harmony, Franco-Vietnamese friendship, and direct rule?"

"Why not? They are dangerous threats to order and security! Normally, it is okay, but when the king comes we must take special precautions against those who advocate direct rule. They want to abolish the God-given powers of the king."

"What about the Communists, Sir?"

"They don't dare to do anything because everyone already knows that they are criminals. But the democracy advocates are different. The government has been tolerant of them up to now, ignoring them and sometimes permitting them to act freely. We are worried that they may try something. Democracy is the enemy of monarchism. It would be even more dangerous if someone was allowed to yell, 'Down with Fascism!' since it would certainly offend the king of Siam."

"What about the Nationalists?"

"No problem because nationalism does not conflict with monarchism."

"In other words, arrest everyone except the Communists and Nationalists!"

"Yes, arrest them all! Pay special attention to anyone who says, 'Long live Democratic France!' and 'Long live the Popular Front Government!'—both slogans will upset the Siamese king."

"What about those who yell, 'Long live the Monarchy!' or 'Long live Siam!' Do we arrest them or not?"

"Good question! I'll ask the chief . . . or . . . on second thought, let's arrest them, too. 'Long live the Monarchy!' will offend advocates of Democratic France, and 'Long live Fascist Siam!' will be seen as dangerous by the Popular Front Government in France."

"Sir, perhaps our policy should be as follows: anyone who greets the two kings by standing as still and quiet as wooden statues, we leave alone. On the other hand, anyone who says anything—even 'Long live France!' or 'Long live the King!'—we arrest on the spot!"

"Hmm. An interesting idea!"

"After all, they are all probably guilty of something."

"That makes a lot of sense. It will certainly contribute to the maintenance of security. But enough already. We must be careful and lower our voices when discussing top secret governmental matters such as these."

After the two agents resolved to conceal the secrets that they had already revealed, Red-Haired Xuân could hear nothing more, only the sounds of chopsticks tapping on bowls. But Xuân had heard enough. Turning back to his table, he found the fortune-teller so engrossed in eating and drinking that he had ignored the entire conversation. Xuân looked at the rapidly vanishing food, folded his arms, and stared at the old man.

When the fortune-teller had cleared the table, Xuân stood up. He was not angry at the fortune-teller's lack of manners because he had come up with a clever scheme to stymie his rival's nefarious plan. Adopting the scornful expression of the upper classes, he signaled for the fortune-teller to follow him.

At the counter where he was paying his bill, Xuân met Dr. Straight Talk together with two young men in elegant European suits. The doctor shook his hand merrily. "This is Professor Xuân, a tennis player. This is Mr. Hải, a very talented tennis player and winner of the Tonkin championship in 1936. This here is Mr. Thụ, tennis champion of both Tonkin and Annam in 1935!"

Xuân shook their hands and bowed low. "I am honored."

"This is truly a great opportunity for opponents—for rival heroes—to get to know each other," Dr. Straight Talk said cheerfully. "The three of you will certainly meet on the tennis court when the king arrives."

Given his displeasure at the doctor's restrained introduction, Xuân was thrilled to spot officers Min đơ and Min toa across the room. That they were without their usual belts, whips, and batons indicated that they were off-duty. Just as he was about to greet them, the two officers spotted Xuân and raised their hands toward him in a military salute.

"*Bông zua me sừ*, Xuân,"[2] they said in unison, "the talented tennis player, the great hope of Indochina!"

Xuân smiled, shook their hands, and turned to introduce them. "Sirs, this is Mr. Min đơ, a policeman of the fourth rank and winner of the Victory Medal. He won first prize in the Tour de Hanoi–Hà Đông and second prize in Tour de Hanoi–Đồ Sơn. He represents the future of the police! . . . And this is Mr. Min toa, winner of the first prize in the Tour de Hanoi–Hanoi Cup, first prize in the Hanoi–Nam Định Cup, the Laundry Boy Cup, and the Melia Jaune Cup. He is the glory of the police precinct!"

Everyone shook hands. Following the introductions, the two officers again saluted Xuân and returned to their table.

Seeing that Xuân was so famous that even the policemen knew him, the Tonkin champions of 1935 and 1936 were extremely worried. A look of fear crossed their faces.

Xuân, on the other hand, was completely content. With his counterplot in mind, he made an appointment to meet with the other two players to discuss a private matter. They were honored, of course, and accepted immediately. Then Red-Haired Xuân excused himself to speak with Dr. Straight Talk in private.

"Doctor," he whispered, "you are a man of great knowledge and talent. I implore you to use your skills to treat a person I know who is in such pain that she . . . may lose her virtue."

"My science can only cure physical pain," the doctor replied. "I cannot do much with spiritual pain!"

"Sir, I beg you to restore the lost chastity of a widow! Otherwise . . . people will mock her mercilessly."

The doctor inquired further about Xuân's strange request, and he related the whole story of his secret love affair with Mrs. Deputy Customs Officer. The doctor was flattered that Xuân considered him such a close friend, and he promised modestly to do what he could. "Okay, my friend. I will employ science to cure physical pain with spiritual medicine."

Xuân said good-bye and paid the check. The fortune-teller was nowhere to be seen.

---

2. Bonjour, Monsieur Xuân (Good morning, Mr. Xuân).

Chapter 19

Imperial Journeys to the North and to the East
◆
The Crime of Cheering "Long Live the King!"
◆
An Antidote for Loose Morals

At two o'clock that afternoon the citizens of Hanoi and people of Tonkin gathered on the sidewalks along the streets between the train station and the residence of the governor-general, the route followed by all important processions. Imperial soldiers lined the roads in a solemn and orderly fashion. The rumors, it turns out, were correct. The king of Siam was undertaking an imperial journey to our country of Nam. People saw pictures of the Siamese king in the newspapers and marveled at his youth. The front pages of all the daily papers published huge seven-column headlines announcing the event: "The Rejuvenation of Vietnam," "A Historic Turning Point: Vietnamese-Siamese Friendship," "Two Kings in One Country," and "Imperial Journeys to the North and East" ("to the North" referred to the direction traveled by our king from Annam to Tonkin; "to the East" referred to the direction traveled by the king of Siam).

Virtually every article referred to the visit of the Siamese king as a "turning point." Royalist papers were especially effusive: "A Special Honor for the Common People of Vietnam: The Siam King Comes to Play with Us!" "Siam and Vietnam: Hand in Hand on the Road to Progress!" Only one paper protested by printing the following on the front page: "Accentuate the Positive, Conceal the Negative! Please Don't Let Us Lose Face!"

Thus the public turned out in their finest clothes to welcome the kings. Many men even wore makeup. The Europeanization Tailor Shop took the opportunity to design a special outfit for women named "Welcome to the King" . . . When the big day came, both Miss Snow and Mrs. Civilization wore the outfit as part of an effort to launch the new design among the upper classes of Hanoi.

Red-Haired Xuân stood with the two other athletes at the corner of Hàng Cỏ Street. Using the intelligence he had gathered at the restaurant the previous day, Xuân was plotting to undermine his rival's plot against him and to secure additional benefits for himself. As part of his counterplan, he had persuaded the tennis champions from 1935 and 1936 (both of whom he was afraid of) to dress in a fashion identical to his. Hence, all three wore white pants, white shoes, sleeveless white shirts, and white caps on their heads.

"Since there are only three of us," Xuân had explained to them, "we must dress differently from the common hordes. We must show that athletes are more than just vain pretty boys."

The two gullible champions fell right into Xuân's clever trap! Little did they know that he was scheming not only to turn the tables on his enemy but to use his enemy's plot against him to do in the other two as well! The sports festival was scheduled to begin the day after the kings arrived. As he was clearly a weaker player than the two ex-champions, Xuân knew it would be futile to rely on talent alone.

The royal cars were slow to arrive, and the crowd began to grow uneasy. Hải and Thụ stood stoically at attention, posing so as to make the muscles in their arms bulge out. Like virtuous noblemen, they stared straight ahead, taking no notice of the beautiful girls watching them from across the street. Pretending that he was borrowing their handkerchiefs, Red-Haired Xuân inserted himself between Hải and Thụ and slipped his hands into their back pockets.

"So, what should we cheer?" he asked innocently, "Long live the king?"

The two champions smiled condescendingly but did not reply. Red-Haired Xuân kept an eye on his back. Finally, he caught a glimpse of his rival's henchman approaching from behind (he was tipped off by the cap, the hair in a bun, and the Chinese shoes). Xuân folded his arms and feigned ignorance as the henchman furtively slipped something into his back pocket and quickly stole away. Moving slowly so as not to draw attention to himself, Xuân pulled the sheets of paper from his back pocket, divided them into two stacks, and, without so much as glancing at them, stuffed them into his two friends' back pockets. Naturally, they thought he was returning their handkerchiefs. Transfixed by the talking flowers on the other side of the road, Hải and Thụ neither noticed nor suspected anything.

Red-Haired Xuân surveyed the crowd looking for Miss Snow's ex-fiancé. Although they were only five people apart, it was difficult for Xuân to spot him because he was wearing a European suit and a pair of sunglasses! He obviously planned to do something bad.

The crowd began to buzz with excitement. The king's car had been spotted, and the hooves of cavalry horses echoed in the distance. Xuân glanced around and saw his lovelorn rival and the old-fashioned gangster positioning themselves a few steps away from him.

"So, which will it be?" Xuân asked his two friends again, "'Long live the king!' or "'Immortality for the king!'?"

Hải and Thụ scoffed at Xuân's old-fashioned enthusiasm.

"*Toa* just imitate *moa!*" one of them said.

The kings' cars were now only a few steps away. People in the crowd swayed back and forth, pointing and talking excitedly. Quick as a water hen, Xuân darted through the crowd in the opposite direction of the procession. After moving about twenty meters, he stopped and looked back.

"Vive la France!"[1] tennis champion Hải yelled out suddenly.

The slogan was immediately followed by several others. "Vive la Front Populaire! Vive la Republique Francaise!"[2]

To the crowd on the pavement expressions of shock were clearly visible on the faces of the governor-general, the resident superior, the king of our country, and the king of Siam. After the procession passed, imperial soldiers refused to let the onlookers dissolve into the street. A phalanx of security agents and secret policemen descended on the section of the crowd from where the slogans had rung out. Following normal procedures, people's pockets were checked for bombs and guns. In the pockets of the two champions, leaflets denouncing Siamese imperialism were discovered and confiscated.

---

1. Long live France!
2. Long live the Popular Front! Long live the Republic France!

The two men were ushered into a squad car and driven to police headquarters.

Since every newspaper in Indochina had come out early in the morning on that day, reliable news about the episode was scarce. Rumors spread among the citizens of Hanoi that the government had arrested two dangerous extremists belonging to the "Sleeveless White Shirt Party." Even the General Athletic Department was unaware that the suspects were actually the two ex-champions who were scheduled to play for the kings the following morning.

The crowd dispersed, and Red-Haired Xuân returned home. Upon meeting Miss Snow and Mr. and Mrs. Civilization, he confidently assured them that the Indochinese Tennis Championship would soon be his.

Just like a real manager, Mr. Civilization urged him to be cautious. "The king of Siam is also a big sports fan. It seems that he has brought along his own tennis champion, who is supposed to display his talents to our French and Vietnamese spectators following the national tournament! You may be confident of victory in the tournament, but you should prepare yourself for the Siamese challenge afterwards. If you can defeat the Siamese champion, it will be a glorious victory for Tonkin, Vietnam, and Indochina!"

"Sometimes we must leave things in the hands of fate," Xuân replied cryptically.

As they walked, Dr. Straight Talk came running toward them. "Mrs. Senior Clerk has invited all her friends and relatives over to her house for dinner," he exclaimed. "We are to celebrate the happy fact that little Master Blessing has stopped sneezing. She has asked me to invite you all."

"You may all go if you wish," Miss Snow replied, "but I will not!"

"But why?" Dr. Straight Talk asked. "Is something wrong?"

"Please do not ask!" Xuân whispered, grabbing the doctor's hand. "Snow is my fiancé."

"Oh, you are so very lucky, my friend!" Dr. Straight Talk answered, with surprise. "Congratulations!"

Everyone shook hands, said good-bye, and promised to meet again soon.

It was strange that Mrs. Deputy Customs Officer had not come out to welcome the kings or to watch the crowds. Xuân, too, was surprised. When he arrived home, he inquired about her absence with Master Blessing, who sagely responded: "No way! No way!" Satisfied that his student's mental capacity had improved, Xuân went off to look for his mother. But, when he came upon Mrs. Deputy Customs Officer, she was unresponsive; she just held her face in her hands and cried.

"This is terrible!" Xuân admonished her. "Please be reasonable! Who can bear such whining! If a love affair with you is this miserable, God knows what marriage would be like!"

To explain her frazzled state of mind, Mrs. Deputy Customs Officer referred Xuân to two recent issues of the *Con Vẹt* magazine.[3]

"Look at these, my darling" she said. "Read the two short novels serialized in these damned issues, and you will understand. I want to sue the bastards . . ."

Red-Haired Xuân read the titles: *The Mistress* and *Uncle Phac-to's Crime*. They were translated versions of *La patronne* and *Le crime au père Boniface*, both by Guy de Maupassant.

Xuân nonchalantly threw both copies of *Con Vẹt* down on the table. "Hey, why don't you read them?" Mrs. Deputy Customs Officer said. "They were obviously written to mock us!"

"Stop being silly! They are translations from the French. I have no interest in reading them!"

"But they seemed as if they were written about you and me!" Mrs. Deputy Customs Officer countered. "It's shameful. I am not at all amused!"

Reluctantly, Xuân sat down and began to read the stories that had allegedly bad-mouthed him. His interpretation of the stories, however, differed from Mrs. Deputy Customs Officer's.

"Anybody who is anybody is bad-mouthed in print," he reassured her. "Not to worry, my dear. In this life the more honorable you are, the more you are denounced in the press. It is only those about whom no one gives a damn that are ignored."

Mrs. Deputy Customs Officer found Xuân's logic persuasive, and she started to calm down. "Of course, you are right!" she said, showering Xuân with kisses. "You are too good to me!"

But Xuân had grown tired of these middle-aged expressions of affection. He pushed her heavily made-up face away.

"How terrible!" he exclaimed.

---

3. *Le Perroquet* (Parrot).

The faithful widow was furious at this rejection. "You no-good bastard! You unfaithful wretch! You have ruined my life, and now you want to get rid of me! It's not going to be so easy with this woman, I'll tell you that! You better watch yourself!"

"Enough, Madame!" replied Xuân, standing up and waving his hand at her dismissively. "You have been very kind! You have a good heart! Maybe I have ruined your life. It is certainly possible! But I think I have found a way to fix it. I have invited a real doctor to see you, not just some quack."

"Oh no!"

"It is true, Madame! A doctor will come tonight who will restore your damaged chastity."

"I don't know what you are talking about!" Mrs. Deputy Customs Officer screamed. "Forget it! I don't need a doctor!"

"Don't be childish!" Xuân admonished her. "You and I, together like that. It's nothing to joke about. If you accuse me of tarnishing your virtue, at least you must give me a chance to put things right."

"Forget it! I'll have nothing to do with it!"

Red-Haired Xuân solemnly raised his right hand.

"If I am joking, let Heaven exterminate my entire extended family! I guarantee that Dr. Straight Talk is going to help you. He's due here any minute!"

"Oh my God!" Mrs. Deputy Customs Officer screamed. "Not Dr. Straight Talk! I'm going to die! I must die!"

The sound of car horns outside the gate put an abrupt end to her tantrum. She looked at the clock. It was seven already, and the guests were arriving to celebrate the recovery of little Master Blessing.

With the single exception of Miss Snow, the party was attended by the entire upper crust of Hanoi society as well as several members of the common people who either knew Mrs. Deputy Customs Officer or had business at the Europeanization Tailor Shop. Little Master Blessing sat in the chair of honor.

After an hour of small talk and eating, Dr. Straight Talk suddenly stood up and addressed the guests. "Ladies and gentlemen . . . We are all friends here. I am putting together a short speech about an issue of great social and moral importance that is often misunderstood. Before delivering the speech in public, I thought I might try it out here first in this much more intimate setting."

There was a smattering of applause.

"Great! Long live Dr. Straight Talk! . . ."

"*Líp líp lo*!" Red-Haired Xuân cheered.

"What is your speech about, Doctor?" someone in the room asked.

"I wish to talk about middle-aged women! Why do women over forty often feel an intense desire for love? Should society make fun of these women? Should they be mocked or not? This issue should be familiar to everyone."

A round of applause followed the doctor's introduction. (Friends of Mrs. Deputy Customs Officer were certain he was planning to play a trick on her.) A wave of anxiety swept over Mrs. Deputy Customs Officer, and her face turned pale.

Dr. Straight Talk stood up and began reading from a stack of papers. "Good evening, ladies and gentlemen. Tonight, I will try to share with you the little that I know about the 'autumn of love'—or, in other words, the growth of lust and desire among those who are getting on in years and allegedly ought to know better. Our society has adopted a narrow and prejudiced view of this phenomenon, perhaps because science has yet to fully explain it. For example, if we see a fifty-year-old man hiring a young housekeeper or taking a concubine, we disapprovingly label him a 'cradle robber' (*applause*). It is even more disgraceful for a fifty-year-old woman to become entangled in a love affair. In such a case people do not hesitate to curse and mock her with cruel words. But we must ask ourselves, Are such attacks proper? Do not old or aging people have the right to enjoy sexual satisfaction? No! No, I say! This is a matter for the Creator to decide, not mere human beings! (*Applause.*)

"In the course of life, there are two typical periods of sexual crisis: adolescence and the time directly prior to the transition to old age. Since the Creator has arranged it this way, there are few people who can avoid these periods. The greater the degree of spiritual crisis that teenagers experience during adolescence, the more confusing will be the autumn of love for 'old people who should be content and enjoy life.' When old men take young concubines (*applause*), they are mocked and ridiculed. Sometimes older women also get involved in love affairs and flirtatious encounters (*applause*). Today I do not plan to pass judgment on these bad things but to explain why they occur.

"In regard to the sexual crises experienced by middle-aged women"—Mrs. Deputy Customs Officer sneezed—"Dr. Vachet has some interesting comments. I will quote from his work so as to show that science can illuminate issues hitherto understood through such shallow and meaningless words and phrases as *corrupted customs, itchiness, flirtatiousness, cradle robbing* . . . According to Dr. Vachet, during periods of sexual crisis, women often exhibit strange and unexpected symptoms. The interruption of menstruation coinciding with the shortening of the temper signifies the onset of physical and spiritual changes that in turn may trigger a complex and intractable desire for sex. Unfortunately for these now easily excitable women, these changes tend to occur after their husbands are old and sexually impotent. What are they to do? Since they are old and wrinkled, it is difficult for them to find young paramours who love them deeply (*applause*). Moreover, few women dare to reject convention and public opinion and discard the virtue that they have been cultivating their entire lives . . . But sex continues to obsess them—to make their faces red and their hearts race.

"Alas! These women try to control themselves even as they are undergoing significant uncontrollable changes: they are often angry, hot-tempered, crabby, bored with life, or newly jealous about ancient episodes involving their husbands. Sometimes they suddenly join mysterious religions or take up superstition and witchcraft . . .

"If the husband is still strong, it may be a great boon for him to have such a wife. But, alas, many times the man does not have the requisite strength. Sometimes he has his hands full just keeping the family warm and well fed (*applause*). There are also many cases in which the husband has passed away and the woman must cope with this period of crisis as a widow (*applause*). If she does not remarry, it is only natural that she will take lovers (*applause*). There are many humorous examples I could cite, but what is important to remember is that they all stem from a single physical condition. The crisis is virtually unavoidable, but, fortunately, it lasts for only a limited period of time. Ultimately, the cause lies in the sex organs themselves: the fact that the eggs lack blood and the uterus ceases to menstruate. This gives rise to a kind of physical chaos that Vietnamese women often refer to as 'the end of the guilt.' Later on, as other organs begin to supply the eggs with the necessary fluids, the crisis will dissipate, and the woman will once again become her healthy self!"

The crowd roared with approval.

Mrs. Deputy Customs Officer recovered consciousness the minute the doctor stopped speaking. Not only did the treatment that Xuân had threatened to apply prove harmless to her status as a virtuous widow, but it put an end to the seemingly endless gossip about her ("the walls with ears and the forest with veins"). Her flirtatiousness now had a legitimate place in the sacred book of saints and sages. She was glad, in fact, to know that she had misbehaved in such a scientific way.

Chapter 20

Red-Haired Xuân Saves the Country
—

Red-Haired Xuân: A Great Man
—

Pity the Father-of-the-Bride Who is not Smacked in the Face

Although even the cheapest tickets cost three piasters, over three thousand spectators showed up that morning to attend the tournament. Hanoi's Rollande Varreau Tennis Stadium[1] was about to mark a historic turning point in the history of sports. Rumor had it that many late-arriving tennis fans could not buy tickets and were so outraged that they chose to die in a sporting way—they committed slow suicide by smoking pure opium into their lungs over an extended period.

The hopes of Grandpa Hồng, Mr. Civilization, Mrs. Deputy Customs Officer, Mr. ILL, and many others were dashed early when Mrs. Civilization suffered a devastating defeat in the women's tournament. Miss Snow tried to assuage her father's disappointment by reminding him that a victory by Xuân could still salvage the family honor. At that moment two Frenchwomen were playing for the French Women's Championship; the supporters from the Europeanization Shop barely paid attention.

Seated among high-ranking civil and military officials from all three governments, spectators could see (from left to right): the governor-general, the resident superior, the king of our country, and

---

1. The Rolland Garros Tennis Stadium.

S. M. Prajadhipok, the king of Siam. Although he wore a European suit, the king of Siam also wore a traditional crown made of gold and pearls.[2] It looked like a tower because each of its nine levels became progressively smaller toward the top. It was supposedly a symbol of the land of a million elephants. Behind the king was one of his German advisors and one of his Japanese advisors, symbols of Siam's rapid progress toward independence. Siam's tennis champion, Luang Prabahol, sat next to him, confirming that the king of the land of a thousand elephants was also a sports fan. The directors of the General Athletic Department of Tonkin were anxious and angry because the final match was only moments away, and still there was no sign of the ex-champions Hải and Thụ!

What to do?

The General Athletic Department sent many people to search for the missing champions but to no avail. Even their families did not know where they were. The world of sports was in an uproar; people were shocked, surprised, worried, and frightened. Nobody knew that both men were lying on the bug-infested interrogation room floor of the Security Police Station. Even the Department of Counterespionage was oblivious to their identity, since all of its agents were tailing the two kings, and there were not enough extra staff members to check the prisoners' identity cards. The General Athletic Department concluded that they had been duped and betrayed. Such behavior was not uncommon among famous athletes. To salvage the afternoon and appease the spectators, the directors of the General Athletic Department invited the champion of Siam to play against Red-Haired Xuân.

The match was announced over the loudspeaker, and the audience applauded enthusiastically. After all, Hải, Thụ, and Xuân were known quantities, but no one had ever witnessed the talents of Luang Prabahol, the champion of Siam! The French and Vietnamese spectators were also pleased because they imagined that the General Athletic Department had planned all along for the champion of Siam to play against Xuân, an underdog who had never won a championship. It was a true slight. Of course, Xuân's manager, Mr. Civilization, was thrilled that his client was to represent Hanoi and defend the honor of the Fatherland against the champion of Siam.

---

2. It is unlikely that the king of Siam would have worn a crown on such an occasion.

The audience cheered and applauded for Xuân. The king of Siam, on the other hand, made a face more furious than had ever been seen before on the face of a Son of Heaven who rules over a land of one million elephants. The obvious weakness of his player from Bangkok struck him like a bolt of thunder. Xuân of Hanoi won the first set 6–1. The king of our country, the governor-general, and the resident superior began to show signs of concern. A crushing victory for Indochina in the sports arena might trigger a diplomatic crisis. Alas! Everything in this world has its pluses and minuses. During the second set the crowd watched uneasily as Xuân began to let up on his opponent. Mr. Civilization grew especially worried when Xuân lost the second set 5–7. The more sophisticated sports fans, however, assumed that he was saving his energy for the final set.

During the first game of the third set both players competed intensely. Luang Prabahol played as well as he could but was unable to gain the upper hand. When the referee shouted 15–30, the king of Siam resigned himself to the imminent defeat of his champion. He immediately pulled from his pocket a map of Indochina redrawn by official Siamese cartographers so that Siam's territory extended past the Hoành mountain range. Ignoring the game, he stared intently at the map. "La guerre! La guerre!"[3] whispered the German and Japanese advisors.

Unaware of what was going on, the French and Vietnamese spectators continued to cheer wildly for Xuân.

"Ca răng! . . . Ca răng ta! . . . A văng ta sê vít! . . . A văng ta đờo!" the referee shouted.[4]

The air was thick with foreboding. Our king, the governor-general, and the resident superior exchanged worried glances. Finally, the governor-general ordered the director of the Indochinese Political Bureau to go find Red-Haired Xuân's manager. Naturally, Mr. Civilization was moved that such a high-ranking government official desired to speak with him in private. They huddled together in an empty corner of the stadium.

"The Protectorate Government and the Imperial Government have an important favor to ask of you," the director whispered. "The fate

---

3. War.
4. Quarante! . . . Quarante à . . . ! Avantage service! . . . Avantage dehors! (Forty! Forty! Advantage service! Advantage outside!).

of our county is at stake. You must ask your client to lose the match against the champion of Siam! In return for forfeiting the honors of victory, you will be compensated generously by our government!"

Mr. Civilization was stunned.

"Just do as I say!" the director continued. "It is very important, and time is of the essence! If Annam defeats Siam in tennis, war will certainly break out! We must follow the Peace Policy of the French Government. Otherwise, the mountains will be covered with bones, and the rivers will run red with blood. I'll fill you in on the details later."

The crowd cheered noisily. "Ca răng, ca răng ta. A vắng ta sẽ vít," the referee repeated. Xuân walked over to the ball boy.

"You must throw the match now!" Civilization whispered urgently to him. "Concede! Victory means death and war!"

The audience looked on anxiously as the score changed from 7–7 to 7–8. There was still hope for Hanoi, but then the unexpected occurred. Xuân lobbed a return so absurdly high in the air that it sailed out of bounds and knocked into the fence surrounding the court . . . 7–9. The crowd booed in disappointment. The military band struck up *La Marseillaise* to congratulate the Siamese champion. The kings and high officials returned to the governor-general's mansion.

The official procession of flag-bearing cars left the stadium, but a large section of the crowd remained behind to see Xuân. One small group of angry fans denounced him bitterly. Another felt sorry for him. Still another shouted: "Down with Red-Haired Xuân!" Grandpa Hồng, Miss Snow, Mrs. Deputy Customs Officer, and Mrs. Civilization were extremely disappointed. Photographers swarmed around Xuân snapping his picture. Journalists began questioning Xuân's suspicious play, especially on the final serve. Did Xuân miss-hit the last ball deliberately? How could a talented player like Xuân, a tennis professor no less . . . have brought such shame upon his country?

Denunciations rang out: "He's a national disgrace! Go back to the cow shed! Go back to the cow shed!"

"A bas Xuân! A bas Xuân! Des explications!"[5] shouted several Frenchmen.

The situation began to deteriorate, and Mr. Civilization and Red-Haired Xuân sought a safe haven on the roof of Mrs. Deputy Customs Officer's car. Following Civilization's advice, Xuân prepared to

---

5. Down with Xuân! Down with Xuân! Explain!

address the angry crowd, now several thousand strong and growing more aggressive by the minute.

Civilization was struck by the gravity of the situation and rose to speak first. "Xuân did not lose because he lacks talent or ability! You can all see as much for yourselves. Please, listen for just a moment, and you will know why my client had to lose." The weightiness of his own words pleased Civilization immensely.

Following suit, Xuân addressed the crowd in a haughty and imperious voice. "People! You do not understand the important reason that I conceded the match to the Siamese champion! Frivolous people! You do not know the profound sacrifice that I have made (he tapped on his chest). You do not yet understand that I have renounced personal fame and fortune to secure peace and order for our Motherland! During these dangerous times it is better to sacrifice one's personal glory—even if it means losing a tennis game—than to risk antagonizing a neighboring country." He pumped his fist into the air!

"For many years the French government and the French people have struggled for world peace. Who knows what will be the outcome of a fight between Vietnam and Siam, but such a conflict will certainly drag the entire world into war! Therefore, I did not compete today so as to win points on a tennis court. Rather, I played to serve the higher diplomatic interests of our government!"

He raised his arm over his head. "I do not want thousands of people to fall victim to war—to fall into the trap of arms merchants!" He lowered his arms. "Oh, my people! Although you are angry with me, I still love and esteem you! Go back to work! Go back to your comfortable lives! Enjoy your peace and security! I do not claim to be some sort of national savior—I have only done what I could to save you from the horrors of war! Long live peace! Long live the League of Nations!"

Using the talents he had developed advertising venereal disease medicine and exhibiting the selfless qualities he had learned running errands for a theater (and with the assistance of Mr. Civilization), Red-Haired Xuân had won over the public just like a skillful French politician. Despite the condescending tone of his remarks, the crowd expressed no resentment toward Xuân. Rather, they admired his pluck for daring to deliver such a speech! After he finished, applause echoed like rain in a thunderstorm. Once again, an army of photographers rushed toward him.

"Long live Red-Haired Xuân!" the crowd roared with approval. "Long live his heroic defeat!"

With a modest gesture typical of great men, Xuân pumped his fists in the air, leapt to the ground, and got inside the car. Off it went among a procession of other vehicles, leaving behind several thousand onlookers in a state of emotional frenzy.

When Grandpa Hồng's car pulled into the driveway, he was so dismayed to see Grandma casually chopping areca nuts that he forgot to clear his throat and spit. Didn't the stupid woman know that a historic event had just occurred? "Haven't you heard about my youngest son-in-law?" he asked her. "My only worry is that he has yet to cause sufficient damage to Snow's virtue."

"Did your daughter-in-law win or lose?" Grandma asked innocently. "How about your youngest son-in-law? Did he win?"

"He lost!" Grandpa Hồng replied, pursing his lips. "But there are different ways to lose! He lost victoriously! He lost in the most glorious way! Madame, do not scold me anymore! Your youngest son-in-law is now a great man—a hero. He has single-handedly saved the country!"

Grandma fell silent as various family members began returning to the house. Miss Snow was already putting on airs! Mrs. Deputy Customs Officer flitted around the house like a water bug. Mr. ILL kneeled down slavishly to change Red-Haired Xuân's shoes. Little Master Blessing did not say, "No way." Dr. Straight Talk congratulated Grandma.

"Grandma, I respectfully offer my congratulations to the happy couple."

"Thank you. We have been planning the wedding for a long time," Mr. Civilization responded.

Grandpa Hồng crawled into bed and demanded the services of the opium servant. Although he seemed to be recalling the excitement of the match, he was, in fact, contemplating the age-old expression "Smack the father of the bride in the face." The meaning and origins of the saying were obscure even to the older generation. Grandpa had long affected a swelled head so as not to be considered out of fashion. Maybe it would swell even more if it were smacked. But who was going to smack him? He punctuated the question in his mind with three imaginary question marks. He told himself that only time would tell, closed his eyes, and tried to forget his frustration.

The sound of a car parking and footsteps approaching the house roused him from his sleep. Everybody looked out the window and saw a uniformed Frenchman enter the house. He had stripes on his sleeves and wore a sword hanging from a gold belt. A wave of fear passed through the house.

The Frenchman greeted the guests politely in a kind of Franco-Vietnamese. "Ladies and gentlemen, I would like to speak with the talented tennis player, Xuân, and his manager . . ."

Mr. Civilization bowed down to greet him and signaled for Xuân to stand up.

"Gentlemen," the Frenchman said in a loud dignified voice, "I am an emissary from the governor-general. I have come to inform the two of you that, because of your selfless willingness to forfeit the match to the Siamese champion, the government would like to award both of you with the Legion of Honor of the fifth rank!"

"Hey!" Grandpa Hồng called to his servants. "Prepare the altar!"

The emissary raised his hand. "Excuse me! But the decision has yet to be formalized in writing. It is perhaps too early for the altar. Please wait a couple of days. Moreover, I also must inform you that it is not only our government that plans to honor you. The imperial courts in Huế and Bangkok each plan to bestow honors upon you that may be distributed among your relatives. They include the Dragon Award and the Medal of Siamese Virtue. In addition, the director of the Indochinese Political Bureau wishes to invite you for dinner tonight. He is looking forward to speaking with you."

Red-Haired Xuân bowed his head low. "We are very honored."

Mr. Civilization also bowed his head. "We are profoundly grateful to the government!"

"Please honor the director of the Political Bureau with your presence this evening. You will be awarded medals for yourselves and your family members. You should prepare at once, and the French government will inform the Imperial Courts in Huế and Siam that you plan to accept. I offer each of you my most heartfelt congratulations. Please excuse me, for I must return to the governor-general."

The manager and the talented tennis player escorted the high-ranking emissary to a huge car, displaying a three-colored flag. The car pulled away, and Xuân and Civilization returned to the house. They were speechless with joy. Grandpa Hồng stood up on his bed.

"Ladies and gentlemen, this is a day of jubilation. I wish to announce that my wife and I have agreed to marry our youngest daughter Snow to Mr. Xuân!"

Everyone clapped with the exception of Mrs. Deputy Customs Officer. Mr. Civilization shook hands with his father. "*Toa* is very kind," he said to him. "Tonight at the director's dinner party *moa* will request a Dragon Award for *toa*."

Grandpa Hồng embraced and kissed his son. "Thank you very much! I am deeply honored! How nice of *toa* to treat *moa* like this."

Xuân caught a glimpse of the sulking face of Mrs. Deputy Customs Officer. The faithful widow had a pathetic lovelorn look about her.

"Let us not forget my female friend here," Xuân added, "She is a virtuous woman. She built the tennis court to support sports and has been especially kind to me. Moreover, she has remained admirably faithful to her two ex-husbands. I wish to announce that I will be asking the Siamese government to award her the Medal of Siamese Virtue."

"Is that okay with you, Father?" Xuân asked his new father-in-law. Everyone clapped their hands and cheered.

"Of course!" Grandpa Hồng replied, "It is well deserved!"

Mrs. Deputy Customs Officer was so moved that her face turned red. She longed intensely to throw her arms around her secret lover and kiss him, but, since she had just been awarded the Medal of Siamese Virtue, she struggled to restrain herself. It was up to her to set a good example for other women.

Miss Snow was hiding behind a curtain, pretending to be bashful about her upcoming marriage. Grandma sat at Grandpa's feet, looking forlorn. She regretted that she had scolded her son, criticized her daughter, and bad-mouthed Xuân. Grandpa lay on his bed, smoking his ninety-sixth pipe of opium and imagining the satisfaction of being smacked in the face.

Before everyone had finished congratulating everyone else, a wave of guests merrily entered the house. They included Officers Min đơ and Min toa, Victor Ban, the monk Tăng Phú from the Lady Banh Pagoda, the old fortune-teller, High School Graduate Tân, the horned senior clerk, and Mrs. ILL. A series of long-winded congratulations echoed through the house.

"On behalf of hotel managers I wish to offer congratulations . . ."

"On behalf of the police, let me convey my warmest regards . . ."

"On behalf of the Buddha, I wish you happiness and longevity . . ."

"On behalf of women, I . . ."

The senior postal clerk whispered a special congratulations to Xuân. "On behalf of horned husbands I pray that you have a virtuous wife."

Gradually, the chorus of congratulations became tiresome. Even Grandpa Hồng grew bored. What did he need with more hollow praise? He longed to be smacked in the face so that his head would truly swell up!

But, alas, another distinguished guest arrived! He wore traditional clothes, and his chest was covered with gold medals . . . Who was this stranger?

"Ladies and gentlemen," he announced upon entering the house, "I am a member of the Association of Spiritual and Ethical Development.[6] I wish to meet with Red-Haired Xuân, a great man in our society . . ."

Red-Haired Xuân frowned and stood up. "I am he. What can I do for you, Sir?"

The man put his hands together in greeting. "Your honor!"

"No need for such ceremony!" Xuân responded abruptly. "What do you want with me?"

"Your honor, our association offers congratulations to you for receiving the Legion of Honor. It is a great honor for upper-class intellectuals. I am here to invite Your Honor to join our association. Your presence will certainly contribute to the spiritual and ethical development of our nation. You are truly a noble person."

"I am not noble!" Xuân replied curtly. "I am a member of the common people!"

"Your Honor," the man continued, "although our association has previously stressed nobility, our new policy is more oriented toward the common people. For example, we have taken to playing *tổ tôm*, a card game enjoyed by many members of the common people."

Xuân was unimpressed. "What in the name of your god damn mother's milk are you talking about?"

---

6. Known as Hội Khai Trí Tiến Đức in Vietnamese, the Association of Spiritual and Ethical Development was a neotraditionalist civic group founded by high-ranking mandarins in collaboration with the colonial state in 1919.

"Thank you very much, Your Honor. I also head a committee that is editing a new Vietnamese dictionary. We have heard that Your Honor often uses common expressions such as 'God damn it' and 'Damn your mother's milk.' Hence, in addition to inviting you to join our association, we would like to ask your permission to add some of your colorful expressions to our dictionary."

"Of course," Red-Haired Xuân replied nodding his head. "If it will please you, I will join your association, and I grant you permission to include those words in your dictionary."

"Thank you very much, Your Honor. This is a lucky day for intellectuals and upper-class members of Vietnamese society. Please permit me to take my leave!" He bowed respectfully to Xuân, nodded somewhat less respectfully to the others, and exited the front door.

Now it was the fortune-teller's turn. He was frustrated because he had been waiting for a long time and had yet to get a word in. Stammering and rubbing his ears, he approached Grandpa Hồng.

"Grandpa, on behalf of fortune-tellers, I wish you many blessings and a long life. May the bride and groom enjoy one hundred years of happiness. I am a very good fortune-teller. The predictions that I made about Mr. Xuân five months ago have all come to pass. He is a talented man with a good heart. His fame has spread far and wide . . ."

"How banal!" snapped Grandpa Hồng. "You only praise what everyone has noted already!"

Pity the poor fortune-teller.

"Father, it is true," said Xuân. "His predictions are very accurate."

But Grandpa was sulking because no one had smacked his face yet.

"Grandpa," the fortune-teller continued, "the fate of your son-in-law is the fate of a hero, of a great man. He will have power, wealth, a beautiful wife, and many children. Xuân is like a precious—"

Tired of the fortune-teller's nonstop ranting and disappointed that no one had yet smacked his face, Grandpa was overcome with an urge to smack the fortune-teller. But, instead, he closed his eyes, coughed in his usual way, grabbed his chest, and moaned: "I know! I know, what a pain! . . . Shut up already!!!"